# HOW TO GET WHAT YOU WANT

## without having to ask

# Prentice Hall LIFE

If life is what you make it, then making it better starts here.

What we learn today can change our lives tomorrow. It can change our goals or change our minds; open up new opportunities or simply inspire us to make a difference. That's why we have created a new breed of books that do more to help you make more of *your* life.

Whether you want more confidence or less stress, a new skill or a different perspective, we've designed *Prentice Hall Life* books to help you to make a change for the better. Together with our authors we share a commitment to bring you the brightest ideas and best ways to manage your life, work and wealth.

In these pages we hope you'll find the ideas you need for the life *you* want. Go on, help yourself.

*It's what you make it*

\* \* \*

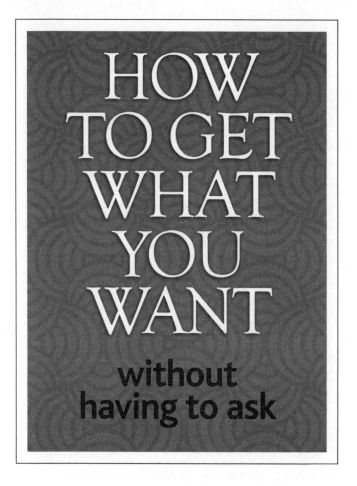

# HOW TO GET WHAT YOU WANT

## without having to ask

# RICHARD TEMPLAR

**Prentice Hall Life
is an imprint of**

Harlow, England • London • New York • Boston • San Francisco • Toronto
Sydney • Tokyo • Singapore • Hong Kong • Seoul • Taipei • New Delhi
Cape Town • Madrid • Mexico City • Amsterdam • Munich • Paris • Milan

Pearson Education Limited

Edinburgh Gate
Harlow CM20 2JE
Tel: +44 (0)1279 623623
Fax: +44 (0)1279 431059
Website: www.pearsoned.co.uk

First published in Great Britain in 2011

© Richard Templar 2011

The right of Richard Templar to be identified as author of this work has
been asserted by him in accordance with the Copyright, Designs and Patents Act
1988.

Pearson Education is not responsible for the content of third party internet sites.

ISBN: 978-0-273-75100-7

*British Library Cataloguing-in-Publication Data*
A catalogue record for this book is available from the British Library

*Library of Congress Cataloging-in-Publication Data*
Templar, Richard.
  How to get what you want without having to ask / Richard Templar.
    p. cm.
  ISBN 978-0-273-75100-7 (pbk.)
  1. Success. 2. Success--Psychological aspects. I. Title.
  BF637.S8T434 2011
  158.2--dc22
                          2011009882

10 9 8 7 6 5 4 3 2
15 14 13 12 11

Design by Design Deluxe
Typeset in 11pt Sabon by 30
Printed and bound in Great Britain by Clays Ltd, Bungay, Suffolk

Textured background on cover copyright oldmonk, 2011 used under licence from
shutterstock.com.

# Contents

Introduction  1

## PART 1 Be the kind of person who gets what they want  4

Know what you want  6
Know why you want it  8
Know how much you want it  10
Want what you get  12
Don't be a fuzzy thinker  14
Know what it takes  16
Work out who you need onside  18
Break big ambitions into chunks  20
Set up some mileposts  22
Celebrate every step  24
Write it all down  26
Analyse your sticking points  28
Set yourself deadlines  30
Check out the back door  32
Don't make excuses  34
Think positive  36
Don't hang out with naysayers  38
Say it out loud  40
Believe in yourself  42
Expect ups and downs  44
Enjoy it when you get it  46

## PART 2 Be the kind of person people want to say yes to  48

Don't fake it – have real confidence  50
Sound confident  52
Look confident  54
Learn to say no  56
Give them an alternative  58
Be a stuck record  60
Be sure you're sorry  62
Say what you mean  64
Think before you speak  66
Be prepared to disagree  68
Control yourself  70
Express yourself  72
Don't use emotional blackmail...  74
...and don't give in to it  76
Treat people with respect  78
Have plenty of time  80
Be likeable  82
Have a sense of humour  84
Be honest  86
Always say thank you  88
Don't do too much  90
Give a bit extra  92
Be generous  94
Praise but don't flatter  96
Be loyal  98
Don't talk behind people's backs  100
Learn to take criticism well  102
Admit your mistakes  104
Get to know people  106
Learn to listen properly  108

Know what you've agreed  110
Pick up the signals  112
Sympathise with other people's anger  114
Don't respond to tactical anger  116
Give other people results  118
Be part of your organisation  120
Work hard  122
Work right  124
Be worth it  126

## PART 3  Help them to say yes  128

Make sure you're getting through  130
And make sure *they're* getting through to you  132
Think about why they'd say no  134
Show you understand  136
Be objective  138
Give them an excuse to make an exception  140
Solve their problems  142
Read the clues  144
Learn what gets them going  146
Use the right words  148
Get the timing right  150
Tell them what you want without asking  152
Don't keep dropping hints  154
Make it hypothetical  156
Ask questions  158
Ask for advice instead of a job  160
Get someone to do the asking for you  162
Tell them you need them  164
Don't rush them  166
Give them what they want  168
Make them think it was their idea  170

Discourage their bad ideas  172
Find out what it will take  174
Get a team behind you  176

## PART 4  And if you really do have to ask...  178

Be clear what you're asking  180
Pick your moment  182
Make a date  184
Know when to put it off  186
Keep to the script  188
Rehearse it  190
Rehearse their answer  192
Don't go on about it  194
Get the essentials on paper  196
Have a bottom line  198
Ask for more than you want  200
Don't make empty threats  202
Think about it  204
Put the decision in writing  206
Be ready to be decisive  208
Don't give up  210

# Introduction

It's easy to look at the world and think that the people who always seem to get what they want are just lucky. Actually luck has only a small part to play. Of course some people have a better start than others, but we all know people from comfortable, even cushy backgrounds who are miserable, and others who started out with nothing and have created a successful and happy life.

So what's the difference between those for whom things always seem to work out and those for whom it's always a struggle? Well, if you observe other people (as I do) you can see that some people know how to get what they want, and others don't. My wife, who is nothing if not focused[1], comes from a decent background but it's a long way from where she is now. Sometimes people tell her how lucky she is to have the lifestyle she has, with a job that fits perfectly round the kids, to which she replies (very politely but firmly), 'Lucky? Luck had nothing to do with it. I planned it this way.'

It's true. She always knew she wanted to live in an old house in the country with cats and dogs and children and a job she could fit round them all. And I'll tell you something else. Before we ever met

---

[1] Bit of a euphemism there, but I think I'll get away with that word.

– eight years before our first child was born – she had the opportunity to go freelance. She knew she wanted kids in the future, and she thought, 'This will be the job I need one day, when the chance for kids comes along' so she took it. You can see why she resents being told she's 'lucky' to have a job she can work round the children.

There's nothing special about my wife's approach. Anyone can do it. You can do it. Forget about luck – if it decides to join you for a while that's great, but you can do without it. It's just a matter of being clear about what you want, and then knowing how to go about getting it. Which is what this book is all about.

There's a common misunderstanding that getting what you want is the territory of the superconfident, those with chutzpah, bravado, oomph, front. I guess that's because those kind of people are comfortable bossing others around and asking brazenly for what they want. But it's not all about that at all. Of course, if you're not as confident or assertive as you might be, you may not like asking for things. Sure, I can understand how you feel. You don't want to put other people under pressure, or maybe you don't want to be told no. Perhaps you're just uncomfortable about baring your emotions to other people when it comes to discussing the things that really matter to you. It's OK, we can work with that.

You see, if you play your cards right, there's often no need to ask directly for what you want. A lot of the skill is in the work you put in yourself in private – the thinking and planning. If you get that right, the job's half done already.

On top of that, you want people to see you as someone they'd like to help and support. If you present yourself as a positive, likeable person, why would anyone say no to you, without a really good reason? And if they do have a really good reason to say no – well, there are ways to deal with that too. Ways of helping them to say yes.

If you're not used to getting what you want, stand by to change all that. It may take you a while to develop all these skills, but they're all achievable and you can start right away. So what are we waiting for? If this is what you want, let's do it.

RICHARD TEMPLAR

Richard.Templar@RichardTemplar.co.uk

PART 1

Be the kind of
person who
gets what they
want

Look around you. Can you see the haves and the have nots? Of course you can. Some people just seem to have everything fall into their lap, while others maybe try just as hard but don't get. We all have good breaks and bad breaks. So why do some people go on to get what they want so often, while others always seem to get the fuzzy end of the lollipop?

Well, it's a lot to do with you personally. If you get the foundations in place, you're much more likely to get what you want most of the time. So before we look later on at the techniques you can use, let's just start by considering how you can maximise your chances of getting anything you decide to go for.

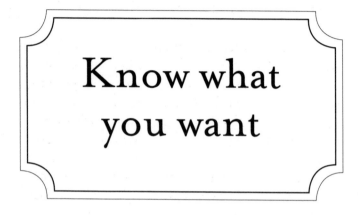

# Know what you want

Pretty obvious really. But hang on, are you really sure you know just what it is you're trying to get? Promotion maybe? A pay rise? Are you desperate for somebody to offer you a new job in their company? Or do you want to persuade your partner to cut down their hours and spend more time with you? Start a family maybe?

Let's take just one of those as an example – say, getting promoted. OK, that's an aim. So what's your problem? If you work reasonably hard the odds are you'll get just what you want, eventually. Most of us gradually work our way up the ladder. Oh, you didn't want it eventually, you wanted it now – is that right? Well, why didn't you say so?

And while we're at it, precisely what job do you want to be promoted to? And at what pay?

You see, the clearer you are about what *exactly* you want, the easier it is to aim for it. Otherwise you may not even know when you've got it. Take getting your partner to work less and spend more time with you as an example. If they come home earlier one night a week will you be happy? Will you have got what you want? Maybe that will be fine. Or maybe you want them to come home at a reasonable time three days a week, or every day, or just one day but to also be up for going out for the evening.

Try asking yourself: 'How will I know I've got what I want on this?' What will be different? What will have changed? How will your life look?

So the very first step to getting what you want is to identify precisely what that want is.

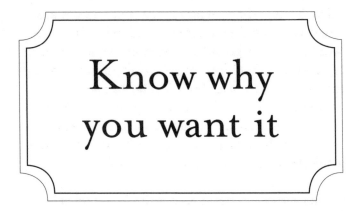

Know why
you want it

So let's go back to that promotion. What's that all about then? Is it that you want to be recognised by the company? Or to improve your career prospects when you move on? Or to make your mum proud? Or because you want the pay rise that goes with it? Or is it just that you don't want that colleague you can't stand to get it instead?

There's a reason for considering this. You see, it might turn out that what you *think* you want isn't actually what you want at all. Suppose you were offered a more impressive job title but without any pay rise or significant increase in responsibility. Would you have got what you want? That's going to depend, isn't it? If what you really wanted was recognition from your boss, it may well be the answer to your wishes. But if you wanted promotion because you needed a higher salary then it's not going to help. In fact a pay rise without a promotion would have been much closer to your goal.

Say you want a better relationship. Why is that? You might think that the answer to this question is obvious. And indeed you might be right. Sometimes it is obvious. But sometimes we don't realise exactly what we want until we've established why we want it. People who get what they want don't take the 'why' for granted. They think it through.

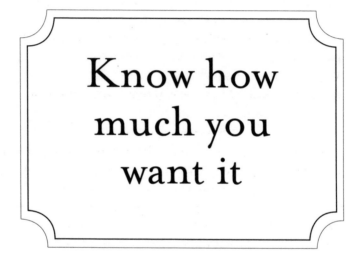

Know how
much you
want it

We want lots of things. Well, I know I do[2]. I expect you do too. So it's important to know what you really, really want. Sometimes we have to play one thing off against another. That's hard to do unless you know where your priorities lie.

Those people who always seem to have what they want... actually they don't. They often sacrifice smaller wants in the interests of bigger ones. They pass up on the promotion they wanted because it would mean longer hours and family time means more to them – that's the thing they really want. Where they were smart was in recognising how much they wanted each thing, and prioritising them.

How much do you want to start a family, for example? Enough to stay put rather than moving to a house in a more expensive area? Enough to give up holidays abroad for the foreseeable future? Enough to put your career on hold for a few years?

No one can have everything. So work out how much you want the particular thing you're aiming at, especially in relation to all the other things you might want.

[2] Starting with a machine that can detect you thinking about coffee and make it before you've noticed you wanted it.

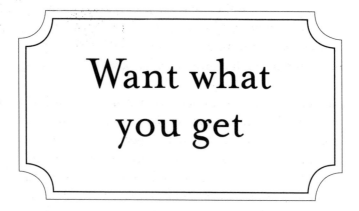

# Want what you get

I have a friend who once went for an interview for a job. To be honest she was driven by desperation – she just needed to get away from the hellish career situation she was in (and fast). She didn't get the job and was absolutely gutted. However, having met my friend, the interviewer decided to bring forward plans to create a completely new role (as well as filling the existing vacancy) just so she could be hired.

She's still working in that job ten years later; it's been that good, and it has taken her in a whole new direction she would never have previously envisaged but one she came to feel was absolutely ideal for her.

I have another friend who met a woman he liked, as a friend, but initially discounted her as a future partner because she wasn't like his previous girlfriends, and there was no stomach churning or massive physical firework reaction. The woman is now his wife, they've started a family and he considers himself to be the most amazingly lucky man to have such a brilliant relationship.

Sometimes you don't know what you want until it happens. You can't always predict what's going to come your way. But if you are open to possibility, and are willing to give things a go and see where it takes you, sometimes it will take you to a place you couldn't have envisaged, but that is perfect for you. It might be that you get something that is not exactly what you originally envisaged as your goal, but you can decide to want it having already got it.

Only you will ever really know whether you get what you want. I'm not advocating settling for second best here. This is not about compromise, it's about attitude. If the point of the exercise – to find work you enjoy, to have a brilliant relationship – has been achieved, it's entirely a matter of perspective.

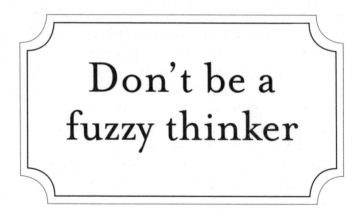

Don't be a
fuzzy thinker

If you want something, you have to go for it. You don't necessarily have to sacrifice everything (sometimes you do) but you do have to make a firm decision to take action. It's no good saying you want to give up smoking if you just carry on lighting up and thinking how nice it would be if you could stop. Do something about it.

I know one person who can't even make a decision about whether to have a cup of tea or a cup of coffee in under five minutes. It usually takes him several years to move house or to hand in his notice at a job he doesn't enjoy. Hardly surprising then if he doesn't often get what he wants.

You have to be firm with yourself. Once you've identified what you want – and decided why you want it and how much – you need to make a decision about whether you're going to do something about it. Commitment: that's what you need. After all, if this is definitely what you want, what are you waiting for?

People who get what they want are generally decisive people. And if you want to do this without having to ask, you need to be doubly firm with yourself. It's OK – decisive behaviour may not come naturally to all of us, but you can learn it. Just jump in with both feet. It gets easier every time.

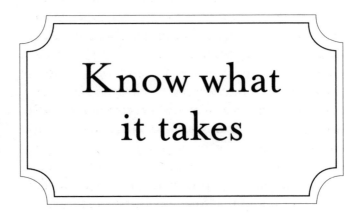

Know what
it takes

So how are you going to go about making things happen and reaching that goal? It won't just happen. You need to make a list (it could be long, it could be very short) of the things that have to happen in order to achieve your aim. After all, if you don't know what they are, how are you going to make sure they actually do happen?

You might need something concrete – to borrow money to pay for a new car or the fancy wedding you want, or to get an appointment with the boss of the company you want to work for, or to find a babysitter once a week so you can go out and do whatever it is you want to do. Or maybe you need to influence someone's behaviour, or encourage them to change their attitude. In that case, what will it then take to change their mind? Whatever it takes, you'll have to identify it. Otherwise how are you going to make it happen?

Look, you have to put something in to get something out. A lot of the work may simply be a matter of thinking, or it might take months of long hard work. But however it might look from the outside, good things don't just fall into people's laps. Not very often anyway. If you want something you have to work out how to get it, and this is the first stage of that process.

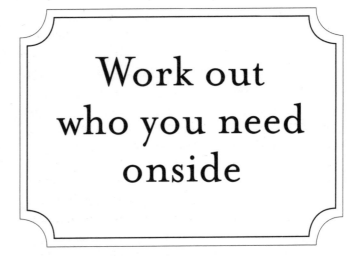

Work out
who you need
onside

You're not alone, you know, and you don't have to do this by yourself. Even if you don't take other people into your confidence, you may need their cooperation. So start by establishing who can help you. They may be an essential part of the team, or they may not even know they're helping you.

Let's go back to your promotion. You need your boss on your side for a start. And very possibly their boss. And maybe some of your senior colleagues. You may also need your partner's support – whether because a promotion will mean a shift in hours, or because you want them to help you practise your interview skills.

Dealing with any kind of life or work problem is going to be a whole lot easier if you have good friends, or your partner again, backing you up. And if your family are really with you they can provide that crucial practical and emotional support. Maybe you also want a network of other people in your situation.

Perhaps you're on your own and would like to meet that special somebody. Do you know anyone who can introduce you to people? If you want to try online or speed dating, would it be a good idea to get advice from someone who has tried it before? (The answer's yes to that one.)

Right, now we're getting somewhere. We're starting to see what you need and who you need, so you can lay the groundwork thoroughly and make this aspiration far more likely to come true.

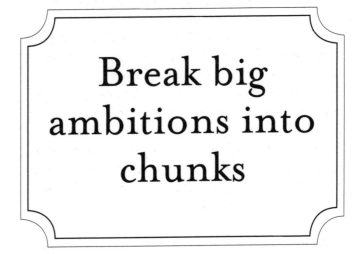

Break big ambitions into chunks

There's a big difference between wanting to buy a little runaround car and wanting a Rolls Royce or a Lamborghini. Sometimes what you want should be achievable in a fairly short time. But other aspirations are too big to take a blind jump at. You need to break them into manageable steps. And the important thing is to treat every one of those steps seriously – think each one through as carefully as you would if they were your eventual goal and not just a staging post.

Did you hear about the bloke in Canada who decided to get what he wanted by trading?[3] He started out with one red paperclip, which he traded for a pen. He traded that for a doorknob and so on. Just kept trading up until he finally got a house. You see, there's no way he could have traded that paperclip for a house straight off, but because he took it one step at a time, he got what he wanted in the end. In his case it took 14 trades. In your case there may be only one or two steps – or there may be many.

Take big ambitions in stages, and treat every stage as an achievement in itself. Otherwise the mountain will be too high to scale and you'll lose heart. In fact, you may well end up with far less than you could have done. If you want that Lamborghini, aim for a few cars of increasing value, impressiveness, coolness, speed, or whatever-it-is-you-want, on your way to the ultimate car.

[3] Check out www.oneredpaperclip.blogspot.com.

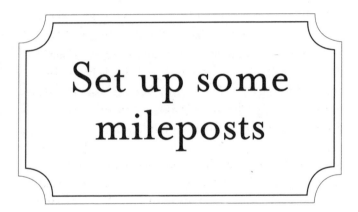

Set up some
mileposts

Not every ambition is big enough to break into chunks. But whether or not yours is, it's certainly worth setting up some waymarkers. These aren't final concrete achievements, but they are steps along the route. So, for example, if you're trying to lose weight you might ultimately be aiming to lose two stone over the next six months. But if that seems a long haul, aim for a more modest point along the way. Maybe losing four pounds by the end of this month, for example.

Not all mileposts have to be so concrete. Maybe you know that in order to get promoted you need to win a particular contract, get your boss to give you more responsibility, find an opportunity to impress the board of management with a valuable self-generated report, exceed certain targets, and so on. Each of these is a step towards your goal.

Starting a language class requires you to locate the class, free up the relevant evening to attend it and maybe find someone to go with you. None of those things is an end in itself, but without them you won't get what you want.

Mileposts are important for two reasons. For one thing they help you to get organised so you can launch your plan more effectively. And for another thing they ensure you stay on track and keep pointing towards your destination.

# Celebrate every step

It's great if you can focus ahead on what you're trying to achieve. But don't forget to look back and see how far you've come. Every time you reach any milepost along the way, you need to recognise the fact, rejoice, celebrate, enjoy your success, bask in the achievement. It may only be one step towards your ultimate goal but, hey, it's one more step towards your ultimate goal. That's a good thing! It's worth enjoying.

Think of it this way. If you've maybe broken your aim down into chunks, and then broken each chunk down into goals along the way, you *want* to reach those goalposts. So when you do, you've got what you want. OK not all of it – not the end objective – but you've got as much as you can get at this stage and you're well placed to move on to the next stage. So you're already a person who gets what they want… even if you still want more besides.

The power of positive thought is huge. Just by consciously acknowledging your achievements along the way, you'll feel more successful. And that, in turn, will make your future challenges seem more achievable. So it really is important to celebrate. Some celebrations may be private and others may be very public – I don't care how you do it so long as *you* realise how well you've done.

So come on – celebrate getting that person onside, or persuading your boss to give you a particular responsibility, or securing an interview, or reaching the halfway point in saving for a new computer or car or holiday or whatever. You're doing brilliantly!

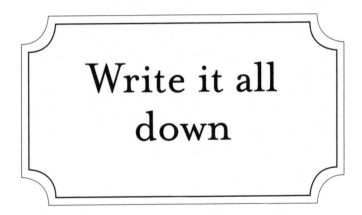

# Write it all down

R ight. Go and get a pen and paper – hurry up – yes OK you can write on this book if you must, I don't mind. OK, now you need to get a few things down on paper[4] before we go much further. Ready?

Write down what you want, and then write down what you need in order to get it. Put down any chunks you need to break your goal down into (smaller wants), and also the more detailed steps along the way (what you need to achieve first).

You're doing this for a couple of reasons. To begin with, you're going to forget it if you're not careful. Anything worth having is going to take some detailed thought and planning and preparing and groundwork-laying. If it's not down in writing you risk leaving out something vital that slows you down or even stops you in your tracks.

And also it seems more real once you have something down in black and white. This is a plan. This is actually happening. This is progress. No longer a dream or a vague wish but a solid, clearcut plan of action.

You see? All those people you thought were getting what they wanted because they were lucky or had good karma or something. Nope. They've just got a pen and paper and they're not afraid to use them.

[4] Or screen, if you really must.

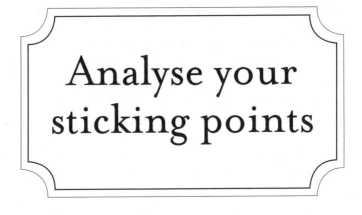

# Analyse your sticking points

Some things are going to be harder than others, right? It's one thing to put aside a bit of money every week in the spring, but quite another to keep saving in the run-up to Christmas, or while you're on holiday. It's easy to persuade your sister to host the big family event, but persuading your divorced parents to both attend is in a whole different league. Meeting your performance targets at work should be do-able, but carrying off that presentation smoothly is a far bigger challenge.

When you look through the list (that you've now written down so you *can* look through it), certain things are going to jump out at you as being much harder than others. These are the ones you need to focus on. I say this because your instinct is often to do the opposite – to ignore them and hope they'll go away. But if you're going to get what you want, focus on them you must. They are the key things that stand between you and what you want.

Look, if you can just overcome these difficulties, you're almost home and dry. The rest is a doddle. So put your efforts into thinking about how you can get round these obstacles more than any others. Work out where the problem lies, what it will take to resolve it, how you can master that.

Anyone can turn up if they're invited for an interview after responding to a job advert. But suppose your dream company isn't advertising and you have to ask for a meeting? That's the bit that's going to be hard. Don't start worrying about your CV right now. Just think about how you're going to get to meet the MD. Is there any way to do it without asking directly, if that seems just too scary? Do you have a mutual contact? Can you write instead of phoning? Or turn up at an event and introduce yourself? Don't sidestep the issue because you don't want to address it, or you'll never get what you want.

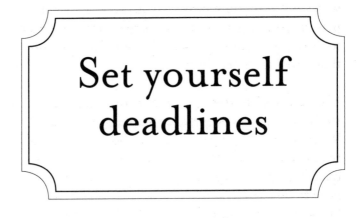

# Set yourself deadlines

Right, we're going to make things happen. Erm... what things? When? Well, you have to put a date by all the things you've listed that you need to do. Otherwise it may never happen. Does this sound a bit like project management to you? Good, because it is. Getting what you want is a project, and you need to plan for it in the same way.

Deadlines, that's what you need. Something to work to. You need to decide when things will happen – or at least the latest date by which they will have happened. Suppose you want your sister to host a family party for your brother's thirtieth birthday.

You know there's loads that needs organising – food, entertainment, invitations – but you need to get your sister to agree in the first place and probably your mum is the most likely person she'll say yes to. So when will your mum next see your sister to ask in person? And when, in turn, does that mean you need to brief your mum? You see, it's not only the obvious things that need deadlines.

Maybe you want to be given more of a marketing role at work after the planned shake-up next year. What will it take to persuade your boss to give you that responsibility? Do you need to gain any extra qualifications or experience first? When would you need to do that? When should you let your boss know what your ambitions are? If you want to produce a marketing-related report to impress your boss, when would you need to do that?

Everything needs a deadline or why would it ever bother to happen? You can probably complete it before the deadline – that's great – but if you let everything run it will never happen at all. And you'll have only yourself to blame.

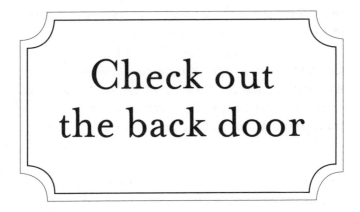

Check out
the back door

Of course there's always the obvious route to getting what you want – such as persuading your boss to let you have a company car – but that's the bit you don't want to have to do. Well OK, let's find another way round it then.

Maybe what you really want is that swanky Mercedes to impress your friends with. But there are other ways to get one. Perhaps you could apply for a promotion to a job that comes with a car. Not likely to happen just yet? Alright then, how about a pay rise (more later on how to get that) and use the extra money to upgrade your own car.

Or you could do some extra work – freelance for your own company or get a second job – to earn the extra you need. Or use any contacts in the motor trade to find a really cheap car for sale, or one you can fix up.

You see, if you think creatively there's often another way to get what you're after. So don't give up – get thinking.

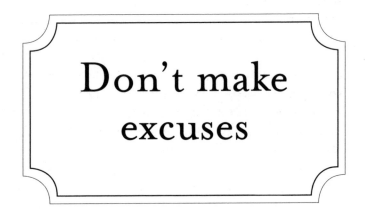

Don't make excuses

I t's difficult when you're trying to deal with people who don't want to cooperate. And actually it's tough trying to meet any kind of deadline if you work long hours. Not to mention the problems of trying to free up an evening when you have kids. Or give up smoking just when life is getting particularly stressful. Or lose weight over Christmas. Or... *shush!* Enough! I've heard them all before!

Look, I don't care if you don't do this. It's not me who wants the new job / better relationship / more attention / white wedding / holiday / girlfriend / baby / fantastic body[5]. Either you want it or you don't. If you want it, you'll look for reasons why you can, not reasons why you can't. Want to know why some people always seem to get what they want? It's because they don't sit around making excuses and hoping it will just manifest out of thin air while they're waiting. They do it despite all the obstacles that could deter them. They get their heads down and they don't take no for an answer.

So let's have no more excuses. If it was easy you'd already have what you want. The whole point is that it's difficult. If we let that put us off we'll never get anywhere. Alright, lecture over. That's better. Pull yourself together and let's get down to business.

[5] OK, maybe I want that last one...

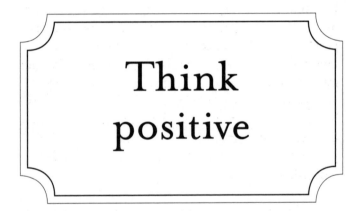

Think
positive

The last point should have shown you where negative thinking gets you. Yep, that's right, nowhere. If what you want is big, or important, or difficult, or daunting, your biggest challenge may be the psychological one. Most wants that are at all realistic are potentially achievable, but if you let yourself be put off you're far less likely to get there. In fact you may never even start. You'll make excuses, procrastinate, avoid the tricky bits and generally never really give the thing a decent shot.

It's important to get yourself into the right frame of mind. A positive frame of mind. Don't give yourself permission to be pessimistic about the outcome. Don't allow yourself to go through scenarios in your mind that involve you failing at this, or being too late for that, or just missing out, or being told you haven't earned / won / got what you want. As soon as your mind starts to head that way, be firm. Tell yourself, 'No.' That kind of thinking is forbidden, banned, *verboten*.

Instead think about your aim, consider all the points you have on your side, reflect on how far you've come and think about how good it will be when you finally get what you want. Remind yourself of all the times you – and others – have got what they want despite obstacles and challenges, and list all the reasons why you should be able to succeed.

Positive thinking isn't something that only positive people can do. It's quite the other way around. Positive people are so because they choose to think positive thoughts.

Don't hang
out with
naysayers

I knew a young man who was offered a job in London. I don't know if you know London, but I can tell you that if you've grown up in the countryside it's a big, scary place. He was pretty daunted by the prospect of coping with the underground trains, finding his way around and sorting out somewhere to live. But the job was just what he wanted and he was really keen.

Until he went home and told his best friend all about it. His best friend was worried. 'How on earth will you cope with the overcrowded Tube trains? Where will you live? You'll never find your way around. What if you can't afford to live? London is really expensive. I wouldn't go there, mate...' and so on and so on.

Well, no surprises, the young man decided not to take the job. He was disappointed, but that was easier than facing up to all those scary possibilities. And where did he go wrong? Well, he knew perfectly well how his friend would react really. It wasn't out of character. He'd have been better off finding someone else to talk to, someone who would have said, 'What a fantastic opportunity! And London's such an exciting place to live. You'll get used to so many people and finding your way around within a couple of days, and you'll have such a great time...'

If you're feeling negative or daunted by the challenges of getting what you want, don't hang out with people who will confirm those negative thoughts. Head for the people you know will big you up and help you to feel positive.

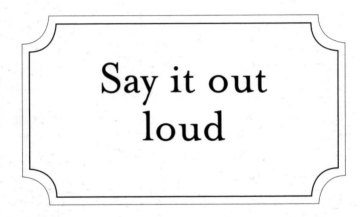

Say it out loud

If you want to believe in something, you need to say it out loud. Tell yourself firmly and unequivocally how it is. 'I deserve a pay rise', or 'I choose to eat healthily', or 'I am making my relationship better', or whatever it is you want. For some reason this is more likely to be successful if you word it in the present tense, and make it positive – don't say, 'I'm not…', but 'I am…'. (Don't ask me why, but that's what research indicates.) So find a phrase that really encapsulates what it is you want to think, and you'll find before long that you do think it.

Whatever it is you choose to say to yourself, say it as often as you like – several times a day at least. This is one of the cornerstones of positive thinking, because you're constantly reiterating positive thoughts. We all know that if you hear anything often enough you start to believe it. Well, this is your opportunity to make that fact work for you.

I really can't say often enough (out loud or otherwise) that getting what you want is as much about your attitude as about what you actually do. Anything that helps to build a more can-do attitude has got to be a good thing.

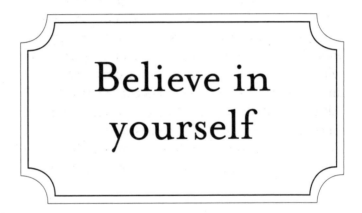

Believe in
yourself

Enthusiasm, optimism, positive thinking – they're infectious. You know that. So use it to your advantage.

Go into any room believing in yourself, and the person you're talking to will believe in you too. And they're ten times more likely to say yes to anything you say.

But it's not just about how other people see you. It's also about how you see yourself. Yep, we're back to attitude again. If you believe that you deserve this, are capable of it, can achieve it – whether it's making enough money to buy a house, patching up your relationship, owning a Ferrari, or becoming a less anxious person – then you'll make it happen. That self-belief will drive you to succeed where you'd have had no chance if you were expecting to fail. Your level of self-belief isn't just about motivation, it will actually change the outcome. And you'd better believe it.

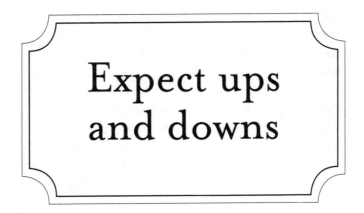

Expect ups
and downs

You know you wrote out that list of things you have to do in order to get what you want? Well, once you start working through it, you'll find that some things go far better than you thought. It turns out that your estranged parents are actually ready to bury the past, at least for long enough to share a table at the family event. They were expecting it, and had already decided to make the day as happy as possible. What a pleasant surprise, after all the ructions you were anticipating.

What you *hadn't* predicted was the roof of your sister's house collapsing a week before the event, necessitating you hiring a marquee at the eleventh hour so the event could be held in her garden instead.

Everything in life has its ups and downs, ins and outs, plusses and minuses. Some bits of your grand plan will go far more smoothly than you dared hope, while others throw up problems you simply hadn't foreseen. And what I'm saying is that that's OK. It's life. You should have been expecting the unexpected. (I do hate that expression, and I'm only using it ironically.)

Don't let the downs drag you down. Face them philosophically. Just say to yourself, 'Ah, this is one of those downs I knew would crop up at some point', and deal with it. Yes it's a pain, but no, it doesn't have to scupper all your plans.

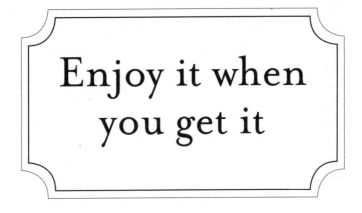

# Enjoy it when you get it

A friend of mine once spent ages saving up for a classic car. I saw him a couple of weeks after he finally got it. And you know what? He was bitching and moaning about it. It kept breaking down, the gears were sticking, the soft top was mildewed in places and its fuel consumption was through the roof. And it wouldn't fit in his garage unless he had a major clearout, which he couldn't face.

What I found particularly absurd about this (as I told him) was that you expect these things with a classic car. And, actually, that's half the point.

They're not worth having unless you're going to lavish love and care on them. He knew that really, but somehow he hadn't taken it properly on board.

My point here is that anyone looking on from the outside wouldn't have seen him as a man who had got what he wanted. Quite the reverse really. So if you're certain that you really do want the thing you're aiming at, make sure you enjoy it when you finally get it. So what if the gears stick? You're now the proud owner of a beautiful classic car. Sit back and take a few puffs on your metaphorical cigar and tell yourself how you didn't get where you are today without hard work.

If you settle for second best, don't check the car over properly before you buy, rush onto the next want before you've finished appreciating this one – your hard work will be wasted. And you'll see yourself as someone who doesn't get what they want when the opposite is true. So relax, enjoy, bask in some glory. You've earned it.

**PART 2**

Be the kind
of person
people want
to say yes to

Most of the things we want in life require other people's cooperation. Whether you want your partner to lend support, your dad to get off your back, or your boss to give you a career boost of some kind, achieving your goals, dreams and ambitions needs someone else to say yes.

And this is where some people have an inbuilt advantage. People just want to say yes to them. There's something about the way they come across that inspires warmth and friendly support. What a skill to have! And it is a skill – not an innate talent you either have or you don't, but a skill that anyone can learn.

The guidelines that follow will tell you the strategies I have observed over the years that help people to get a positive response. And what's more, not only do they help you achieve your aim, they also make you enjoyable to be around and help you to get more pleasure out of life and out of other people. They are an end in themselves, as well as helping you to reach your goal.

# Don't fake it – have real confidence

O h yeah, and how exactly are you supposed to do that? If you're shy or anxious, it's all very well saying 'Be confident!' but that's not how real life works is it? You can't just turn it on. So why even bother telling you to make it real?

Hang on a minute and hear me out. Confidence is all about knowing what you're doing. So it stands to reason that the better you know your 'script' the more confidence – genuine confidence – you will feel. You just need to think through what you're doing and be clear about it.

Suppose you're one of those people who hates the whole 'do I or don't I' thing when it comes to handshakes. What if you don't know whether to offer a hand or not? Hang on, who put the other person in charge of the script? You just have to decide that you're doing the handshake regardless, and then as soon as you greet the other person you firmly put out a hand with a broad smile. See? You just wrote the script, and you know exactly what's in it. And you come across as being confident. So you win all round.

If you know you find meeting and greeting hard, just have a script ready and planned before you get there. Practise in a mirror. Rehearse the moment in your head – play it through as if you are watching it happen. Decide whether you'll shake hands or kiss on both cheeks, or whatever, and have a few lines of greeting ready, or a couple of questions prepared to get a conversation going. You might not feel confident about absolutely everything, but you will feel confident about those crucial first 10 minutes.

It may feel like you're going through the motions slightly the first couple of times you do this, but believe me it will quickly become a habit, and the confidence soon will be as real as it looks.

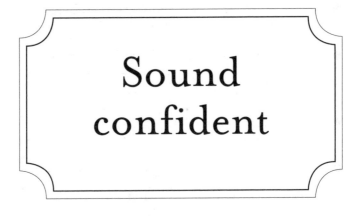

# Sound confident

Confidence sells. It sells you. If you're confident other people will feel they can trust you to do what you say you can, they'll be inspired to rely on you. Suppose you want to win a tricky pitch at work. If you go in mumbling and looking at your shoes you've given yourself a far harder job than if you start off smiling and speaking clearly. Especially if your competitor is slick and self-confident.

It's the same with your boss and your colleagues. Come across as shy and unsure of yourself and they won't be too sure of you either. Confidence is contagious. If you have it, others will feel confident in you.

The way you talk is a huge part of your persona, so here are some quick guidelines for sounding more confident:

- Speak clearly without mumbling or speaking too softly.

- Decide in advance how you're going to express yourself so you know what you're doing when the time comes.

- Practise any really tricky conversations in advance, with a friend or in front of a mirror.

- Use positive language: not 'I think I should be able to', but 'Yes, I can do that'.

And remember, once you're in any kind of meeting you should be thinking about the person you're with, not about yourself. So at the first sign of self-consciousness, give yourself a swift talking to and remind yourself to focus on your companion.

Look
confident

G ood, you're sounding confident and greeting people with a firm handshake or a kiss on the cheek, or whatever you've decided is appropriate. Now then... you need to make sure that your body language matches your confident voice.

I know you don't want to be worrying about body language while you're trying to cope with a nerve-wracking or important meeting. So make it a habit straight away for every encounter. That way you won't have to think about it after the first couple of weeks, and it will become second nature. People don't say yes to shy, uncertain looking people who seem to be coming across a bit less diffidently this time. They say yes to people whom they think of as being consistently capable and sure of themselves.

Look, the aim is to become someone who always behaves in a confident manner. That way, any time you need anything from anyone they'll see you in the best light before you've even had to ask. So make eye contact, look interested and adopt an open and relaxed posture. This isn't difficult – arms by your sides or in your lap, not tightly folded or hands blocking your face. Sit back in your chair and don't perch nervously on the edge of it – that sort of thing. Study other people to see who seems relaxed and confident and who doesn't – and why.

So now you're confident, you're friendly, you're self-assured, you're warm... how could anyone say no to you?

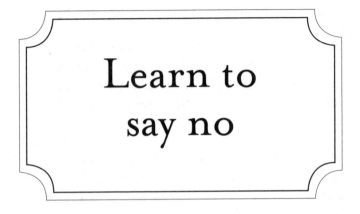

# Learn to
# say no

You'll struggle getting people to say yes to you if you can't say no to other people. Doesn't sound fair, does it? But you don't necessarily have to say no to the same people you want a yes from. The point is that often what you want requires time. That's a commodity that's very hard to come by if you can't say no. Or maybe you need a peaceful life (don't we all), perhaps because you're under particular stress at the moment, and you really don't want anything difficult or complicated dumped in your lap.

You know that expression, 'If you want something done, ask someone who's busy'? That partly works because the people who are busiest are usually the worst at saying no, so they'll always say yes to you. Listen carefully: you don't want to be that person.

Now don't take this as an excuse never to do anything for anyone. That's not what I'm saying. I just want you to do things for people for the right reasons, and not because you couldn't bring yourself to say no to them.

It's really important that you grasp the connection between saying no and getting what you want. I'm not pretending it's vital in every last instance, but there are lots of things that you'll struggle to achieve if you don't have a clear head or a clear slot in your diary. How are you going to organise that group holiday, or clear time for that evening class, or write the report that will wow your boss, or find time to meditate, or whatever, if you're running around desperately trying to do all the things you promised other people just because you couldn't say no?

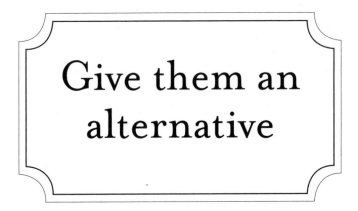

Give them an
alternative

People who don't like to say no generally feel that it's rude or unkind to turn people down when they're asking for something. It just doesn't feel right saying no – you feel you should be trying to help, not obstructing.

OK, fine. So you can still help them. Just don't do it by saying yes. That may be what they think they want, but actually it's not. Suppose a neighbour asks you to babysit and you just don't have the time. Do you feel you're letting them down if you say no? But you're not… because actually they don't need *you* to babysit. They just need *someone* to babysit. If you can help them to a solution that doesn't involve you, then everyone gains.

So you could tell them, 'I can't, but have you tried Julie?', or 'I really can't tonight, but I could do next Wednesday if that helps?'.

Suppose a colleague asks you to cover so they can take a day's holiday next week. You're too busy, but you can still help: 'Not next week, no. I could cover for you after the 25th though'. Or, 'I've got too much work on, but I can sort out your orders at the same time as mine if that helps'.

You're perfectly entitled just to say no of course. I'm only trying to help you here if you have trouble doing that. Also, if your neighbour or colleague goes away feeling that you've helped them – even if you haven't actually said yes to their original request – they're more likely to cooperate next time you need their help to get what you want.

# Be a stuck record

Everyone else doesn't necessarily care as much as you do that you get what you want. How much time do you spend helping other people achieve their aims? I hope you sometimes help, but your real focus is your own stuff surely? Well it's the same for everyone else. They won't all be as focused as you, and they may need reminding.

Come to that, you may need reminding. When work is going well, the sun is shining, no big bills have come in lately, your relationship is going smoothly and there are no clouds on the horizon, it's easy to let things ride. Suddenly you realise that months have gone by, or that you're about to hit problems, and you still haven't got what you want.

So keep reminding yourself, your partner, your boss, or whoever needs to know that you haven't taken your eye off the ball. Remind your boss every few weeks that you're keen to find a role where you spend more time with customers. Keep asking your partner (without nagging) how they're getting on with reducing their hours at work. Make sure your sister is on the case with the plans for that big family event, and check what she needs your help with.

If you don't do this how will anyone (yourself included) know that you haven't changed your plans, and that this is still really important to you?

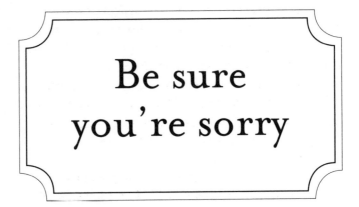

Be sure
you're sorry

S ome people are programmed to apologise no matter what. Just to keep the peace, I suppose. I don't really know – it's not one of my traits frankly. But I can see that it's intended to be conciliatory, which should in theory be a good thing. But it's not good to do it to excess. I know people who say 'sorry' when someone walks straight into them, and take the blame for a mix-up that was clearly caused by the other person not listening, and apologise for serving up 'burnt' food when no one had noticed it was a bit brown on top, and say sorry for delivering a report late when the brief was changed two days before it was due.

If it's not your fault, don't apologise. You don't have to blame anyone else, you can express regret that things have turned out this way, you can acknowledge the mess-up, but don't actually say sorry when you've done nothing wrong.

What does this have to do with getting what you want, you may be wondering. Well, I'll tell you. It's back to that confidence thing. People are far more likely to feel confident in you, respect you, trust you, if you come across as being reliable, confident and trustworthy. That's not exactly rocket science, is it? So if you keep apologising you give the unconscious impression that you keep making mistakes. Why would your bank manager give you a loan, your boss give you a promotion, your dad lend you his car, your mate go on holiday with you, or your neighbour let you take three foot off the top of the hedge between your gardens, if you keep messing up?

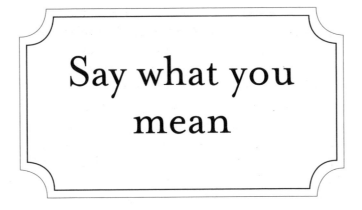

# Say what you mean

I once heard someone offer an under-assertive friend a favour and the friend said no in such a roundabout fashion that the person actually thought they'd said yes, and did it anyway. The friend was annoyed at them doing the opposite of what they'd said – having simply not realised how obtuse they had been. Here's how the conversation went. Let's call them Sam and Ali:

Sam: 'I'm just taking Jess down to the park to play on the swings. I could take Hester along if that's OK with you?'

Ali: 'Well, that's a very kind offer. You know, I'm funny about it. I always think I should keep an eye on her myself. But I'm sure I'm being silly. I mean, what's going to happen? I know it ought to be fine.'

Ali meant no, but Sam heard yes. Ali could have simply said no, but she was worried that this would seem like a rude rejection of Sam's offer, so she wriggled around trying to justify it so much that she didn't actually say no at all. In the event, Ali disappeared into the kitchen for five minutes and when she came back she panicked because she couldn't see Hester anywhere. I told her Sam had taken Hester and Jess to the park. Ali was appalled that Sam would do that when she'd said no. But neither Sam nor I had heard her say no.

So there's a little moral tale for you[6]. If you're one of those people who hates saying no outright, get over it. You can still explain your choice if you feel the need, but make sure you say no unequivocally at the start.

---

[6] With a happy ending – Hester had a lovely time at the park.

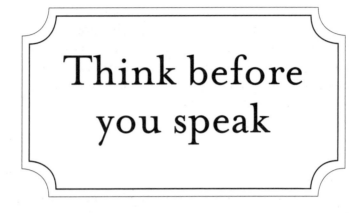

# Think before you speak

Maybe you're not under-assertive. Perhaps you know that far from pussyfooting around, you can come across as being a little brusque. Maybe it's your choice of words, or maybe it's just your manner. Or both. Are you the type to call a spade a spade, or do you intend to be polite and it sometimes just comes out wrong?

Either way, you must have noticed that it doesn't help you get what you want from people. If someone is going to say yes to you, you want to make it as easy as possible for them. In fact you want to make it hard to say no. You want to make them like and respect you so that they want to support you, and to express your request in such a way that it would seem churlish to refuse.

So if you have anything to say that might cause offence or rile someone, catch yourself before you start the conversation and remind yourself not to be personal or to apportion blame, and to concentrate on the situation and not on the people. And promise yourself, if necessary, that once you've made your point you'll shut up.

This is a wise rule if you're going to ask for something, but this book is primarily about getting what you want without having to ask. So I'm not only talking about direct requests – I'm talking about all your dealings with people whom you want to be well-disposed towards you. If you unintentionally make your colleague feel small at this week's meeting, they're much less likely to offer to help you out next week when your workload gets heavy. If you sound irritable when your neighbour asks you to babysit, they're less likely to offer to hold the fort so you can go out.

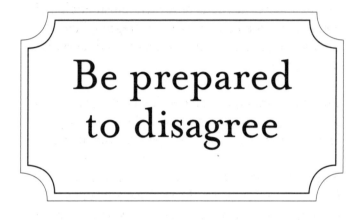

# Be prepared to disagree

Sometimes you have to say when you think someone is wrong. This is about earning respect (and people are more likely to say yes to people they respect – aren't you?). If you can argue a case clearly and without rancour, people will have time for you and will want to listen to your views in future, since you clearly express your own thoughts rather than parroting what you think they want to hear.

It's also about being on the right side. Sometimes you actually believe that someone is arguing for a course of action that you consider morally or ethically unacceptable, and when that happens you have to say so. Suppose there's a case of pilfering in the office and everyone is giving Ella the cold shoulder because they think she's the culprit. But you can see their evidence is purely circumstantial, and you're concerned that they're mistreating Ella. You can't keep quiet about it – you have to disagree with their stance.

Anyone reasonable should welcome disagreement so long as it's expressed in the right way. Yes I know there are always a few people who aren't reasonable, but at least you can make sure you've done your best, and anyone listening will think better of you for it. The key to disagreeing nicely is to disagree with what the person is saying, and not with the person themselves. I know this sounds like a technicality, but it makes a lot of difference to how the other person responds.

You want to avoid direct criticism of the person themselves, so don't say things like, 'No!', or 'You're wrong', or 'You've got the wrong end of the stick there'. Aim to comment on what they've said, and express it as an opinion, however firm an opinion: 'I don't think that's the way it works', or 'I'm pretty certain we'll come adrift if we do that'. You see? You're concentrating on their line of reasoning, not on them.

Control
yourself

W hat is it that makes some people more difficult to deal with than others? I'll tell you, and you'll realise you already knew it really. The thing that gets in the way of making all interactions straightforward is emotion. Negative emotion to be specific. And the more extreme the emotion, the more it gets in the way. When the person you're dealing with is angry, upset, nervous, hurt, disappointed, touchy, stressed, frustrated, resentful, anxious – that's when it's hardest to get the result you want.

And guess what makes things twice as tricky? Yep, that's right: when both of you are emotional. Two upset, angry, resentful, worried people will double your problems, if not worse. So the first thing you can do to ease those emotionally charged conversations is to make sure that you have your own emotions under control. Look, I'm not talking about whether your feelings are justified here, I'm just talking about how to actually get the result you want.

Of course I know that isn't always easy, but stay focused on what you want to achieve and recognise that keeping calm is the best way to achieve it, and that should help you to keep a lid on it. If you really can't stay cool, just walk away until you can trust yourself with the conversation. There are plenty of ways to deal with other people's emotions, but you'll struggle to manage any of them until you have your own under control.

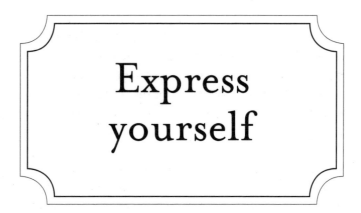

Express
yourself

I just said that you need to control your emotions. But that doesn't mean you can't ever express how you feel. Just express it in words rather than by demonstration. Of course there are times when it's important to let someone know that you're disappointed, or angry, or hurt, or frustrated. They are more likely to give you what you want if they understand how you feel. However, it won't help if you shout, or sulk, or burst into tears.

The way to let someone know that you feel angry is blindingly simple. You say, 'I feel angry'. That's so much better than yelling at them. No one wants to help someone who intimidates them – or puts them down, or makes them feel small, or puts emotional pressure on them, or makes them feel uncomfortable. So don't do those things to people if you want them on your side.

In fact, to take it one step further, say 'I feel angry when...' and then explain what the problem is. This phrase is handy because it's not accusatory – you're focusing on the other person's behaviour and not on them personally. No one wants to be told, 'I feel angry because you're being unreasonable / because you won't listen / because you're putting your interests first'. Much easier to hear, 'I feel angry when I feel I'm not being heard / I feel my interests are being ignored'. It's just a less confrontational, more constructive way to get the other person to listen to you.

Don't use
emotional
blackmail...

Nobody likes being emotionally blackmailed. Some people may give in to it, especially if assertiveness isn't their middle name, but they still know you're doing it. And given half a chance they'll say no to you. Personally I'm pretty intolerant of emotional blackmailers, and even if they have a valid request I find myself wanting to refuse them because I object to being manipulated.

'I'll be in real trouble if you don't help me with this…'. 'Please can I take Friday afternoon off? It's my little girl's ballet show and she'll be so disappointed if I'm not there…'. 'Come on, let's go out tonight. I've had a miserable week and I really need to get out, and there's no one else I can go with.' All of those requests are reasonable if they're expressed without emotional pressure. It's fine to explain that you want the afternoon off for your daughter's ballet show, but not fine to lay on the emotional stuff – implying that if your boss says no they'll be personally responsible for your daughter's misery.

Emotional blackmail is a sly and underhand way to try and get what you want, and my experience is that people who use it may be successful this time, but in the long run they lose out. I wouldn't want to be that kind of person, and I hope you wouldn't either.

Besides which, it won't actually get you what you want in the end, and people will be likely to see you as someone they'd like to say no to, even if they can't always manage it.

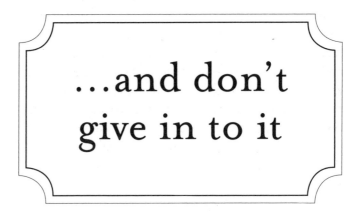
...and don't
give in to it

Y ou need to avoid being on the receiving end of emotional blackmail too. Otherwise you'll end up saying yes to things you don't have the time or the enthusiasm for, just because you've been guilt-tripped into them. Some people, myself included, find this avoidance quite easy. Emotional blackmail irritates me and I give it short shrift. But I know that if you're not very assertive, or you're susceptible to guilt, it can be hard.

The first thing is to recognise it. If you're feeling guilty or uncomfortable about the way you're responding to someone, ask yourself if you're being emotionally blackmailed. If the answer is yes, focus on that fact and not on the guilt they're trying to engender in you. Listen, emotional blackmail is not responsible, adult behaviour. It's unfair and it's manipulative and people who do it don't deserve to get what they're asking for, even if their request is otherwise reasonable. They've disqualified themselves by cheating.

Now just practise whatever technique you have for saying no to them, such as the stuck record technique. Sometimes it can help to challenge them, especially if you can do it with humour: 'Careful now, or I'll think you're trying to emotionally blackmail me...'.

And if that doesn't help you to resist, think about this: every time you give in to emotional blackmail you encourage that person to do it again. So you're partly responsible for the discomfort of the next person who gets guilt-tripped, and the one after that... or am I just emotionally blackmailing you now?

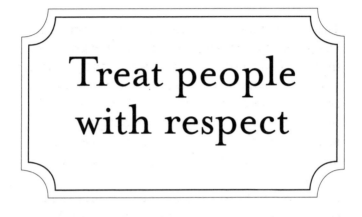

# Treat people with respect

Everyone deserves respect, and more to the point everyone wants it. If you remember that, people will be far more likely to be on your side, to want to help you when you need it.

How many neighbours, bosses, family or colleagues have you encountered who make you feel unimportant at times? Maybe they don't bother to listen when you speak, or perhaps they ignore you because you're junior to them, or they expect you to do things for them without asking properly, or they never bother to thank you for anything. I had one boss who used to take credit for all my ideas. I know people who'll shout at you just because they disagree with you. I had a colleague who wouldn't make me a cup of coffee because she considered that I was slightly junior to her.

Then again, I once encountered an important client who insisted on making me coffee on the grounds[7] that I was much busier than he was at that particular moment. I've had other bosses in the past who credited my ideas (one who only did so when they turned out right, and took the rap herself when the ideas were duff), and neighbours who have brought me gifts to thank me for the simplest of favours.

I know which of all those people I'd want to help out and which I wouldn't be bothered about. It's especially important to treat people with respect as you become more senior – at work, in the family, as a school parent, or a local resident. People are especially sensitive to being ignored or put down by people they see as being senior. So even if you mean no disrespect but are just preoccupied or busy or in a hurry, you need to make sure you never forget to show people that you've noticed them.

[7] Sorry – couldn't resist the pun.

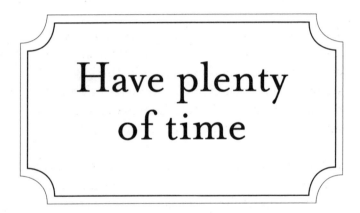

Have plenty
of time

I used to work with someone who was always in a hurry. Whenever she phoned she was on a railway platform waiting for a train, and had to cut you off when the train came in. Or she'd be cooking dinner whilst she talked, and had to put you on hold while she checked the oven. Or she'd be at the school gates and she'd have to go because her son was just coming out. And that's when *she* called *me*. If ever I called her (which I tried to avoid because I found her so difficult to hold a conversation with), I'd be asked to call back later.

The net result of all this was that she gave everyone the impression that they were less important than everything else in her busy life. You always came second to the train, the oven, her son (OK, maybe that last one is fair). It was disrespectful and irritating and infuriating and patronising.

Obviously I know there are times when you really are busy. There's no need to initiate phone calls (or other contact) at those times and then cut it off abruptly. By all means have times when you flag up at the start that you're not free to talk. But make sure there are also plenty of times when you are available for a natter over the garden fence, or with a cup of tea, or by the photocopier. Those are the times when people get to see the real you, and when you can show – just by giving them your time – that you value them. Those are the things that will get people on your side, not to mention being beneficial in themselves because both of you will feel better for it.

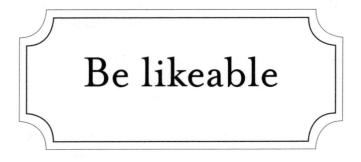

# Be likeable

I know this seems obvious, but if people like you they'll be far more likely to want to help you, preferably before you've even had to ask. It's how *you* feel about other people after all, isn't it?

Being likeable really shouldn't be that hard. You don't have to be the centre of the party, everyone's best mate. You can be quiet and likeable too, you know. In fact, if you think about it, you probably like several people you don't actually have much in common with, or even find slightly irritating, so long as the irritation is harmless – talking a bit too much, or being a bit too giggly and childish, or never sitting still long enough for a decent conversation.

Being likeable is really about being straightforward, easygoing and friendly. A warm smile, a cooperative manner, no sulks or manipulating or temper or negative emotional outbursts. On top of that, aim to be a 'what you see is what you get' kind of person. You say what you mean and there's no bitching behind backs or deceit or arrogance. Think about people you consider likeable – not your best friends but people you know less well and just find that you like. You'll probably find that they all fit that broad picture – straight-up, easy to chat to, good listeners (their conversation isn't all about them), and you don't feel uncomfortable that you're about to say the wrong thing, or that they're not all they seem.

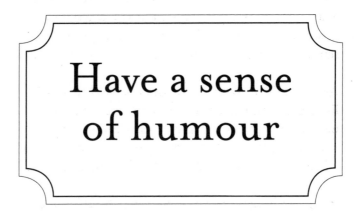

Have a sense
of humour

I'm not sure you can just acquire a sense of humour. Sadly, you can't go out and buy one. Everyone's is different and some are more obvious than others. Some of us have more of a sense of fun than a sense of humour. That's OK. What I'm saying here is that whatever your sense of humour, let it show – at least so long as it's not catty or cruel.

Some people seem to feel that being humorous somehow undermines their authority or seriousness. They put their sense of humour away when they're at work, or sitting on the parish council or the school governors' committee.

As far as I'm concerned, laughter is what makes life worth living. And the more you can make other people laugh, the more well-disposed they'll be towards you. And that's what you're aiming for. Make people laugh and they'll do anything for you.

It's not only that though. The thing about humour is that it's so distinctive: each one of us has such a unique sense of humour that the more we use it, the more it defines our personality – in a positive way. When you shut down your humour you lose a large chunk of yourself along with it. So let it all out, don't be afraid to see the funny side of things, and help others to see it too.

Be honest

You know perfectly well that everyone prefers dealing with honest friends and colleagues. The problem is that most dishonest people are under the delusion that they're getting away with it. If everyone thinks you're honest, well, that's as good as actually being honest, isn't it? Leaving aside the morals of the question, then yes – it probably is just as good. Except that everyone doesn't think it.

Look, I'm not talking about occasionally blaming the traffic for being late when actually you know it was your own fault for cutting things a bit fine. I'm talking about premeditated dishonesty in order to achieve what you want. Getting ahead by deception. Using lies to wriggle out of responsibilities. Adopting untruthful means to further your own ends.

Don't imagine for one minute that you're getting away with it. For sure, you may get away with individual instances. You may even be clever enough to make it work repeatedly. But other people can sense you're not honest, and that will deter them from helping you. Maybe it's your body language, or maybe you're just a bit too good to be true, or perhaps there's something small you've overlooked. They may not be able to pin it on you, they may not have any proof – or even any evidence – but they will simply know that they don't quite trust you.

Far better to live the kind of lifestyle that doesn't require you to lie, cheat, deceive or manipulate. Just be honest – what's the problem with that?

Always say
thank you

I was brought up always to say thank you, and I would feel really uncomfortable if I didn't, in the same way I'd feel unpleasantly odd if I didn't brush my teeth as soon as I got up. Actually my mother, who inculcated this habit in me, was once given two black marks at school by her teacher – the first one was for bad behaviour, and the second one was for being so cheeky as to say thank you for the first one. My mother had explained that she'd been brought up always to say thank you when she was given something. The teacher didn't appreciate my mother's sense of humour.

My mother was right though (well, in principle anyway). We may not always notice when we should thank someone else, but we certainly notice when we aren't thanked. So don't, for goodness sake, leave other people's contributions unacknowledged. It doesn't matter how small they are – no one's going to complain that they didn't want to be thanked.

Thanking people makes them feel good, it makes them feel warm and appreciated and cared about. It makes them feel it was worth the bother. Surely giving someone that kind of feeling has to be worthwhile in itself. And, on top of that, it makes them feel they'd be happy to do something for you again, since they know it won't go unrecognised.

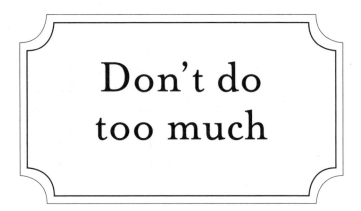

Don't do
too much

S ome people can cope with anything. The world can fall apart about their ears, and somehow they just keep going. They manage a busy job, maybe a large family, plus they volunteer for a couple of charities, sit on one or two committees, and still find time to play tennis twice a week. They are clearly among the world's copers, and they don't seem to need any help or backup to get it all done.

So no one offers them any support. Obviously. In fact, if you really want something done, they're the ones to ask.

All of which is great, unless you happen to be one of those people – and you want some help. You won't get it, you know. Everyone will have decided that you don't really need it. Presumably, as you've actually asked, you could maybe do with a bit of backup in an ideal world, but they needn't feel any obligation because you don't actually *need* them. You'll cope. You always do.

So what's the moral of the story? Well, if you need other people to help you get what you want, don't give the impression that you don't need help. Drop the urge to look as if you can handle anything, and admit to a bit of human frailty now and again. People will probably like you all the better for it. People who can handle anything on their own are a bit scary really.

Give a bit
extra

This is a great strategy – I love this one. I enjoy the look on people's faces when I deliver more than I promised. It makes me feel good and it makes them feel great and everyone gains. How cool is that?

The principle is simple: whatever you say you'll do, do a little bit more. When you babysit your neighbour's kids, do the washing up that you find in the kitchen too. If you say you'll deliver your report on Thursday, deliver it on Tuesday. If your partner expects you to buy them dinner on their birthday, give them a dozen roses as well. When you borrow you dad's car, put it through a car wash before you return it. When your friend wants company after a bereavement, take her a couple of meals for the freezer at the same time.

We had a Christmas visitor a couple of years back who gave us a lovely thoughtful present in return for her Christmas dinner. Not only that, she's a very clever seamstress and noticed that the cats had badly torn one of our cushion covers. She insisted on taking it away with her and repairing it, and it arrived back in the post within a few days looking as good as new. What a generous gesture, and all the more appreciated on our part because she'd already thanked us amply.

You see? It's fun coming up with things you can do to make people's lives that bit brighter than they're expecting. It's wonderful seeing them realise that they're cared about and valued. It's bound to make people want to go the extra mile for you but, to be honest, it would be more than worth doing regardless.

Be generous

F or some reason when we talk about someone being generous we tend to imply that they're willing to give or share material things such as money or possessions. That's certainly a laudible attitude, but not all of us have enough to share, and not everyone needs to share with us. But we do have other things we can be magnanimous with.

How about your time? Are you generous with that? If someone asks you to come to a meeting, or spare them a couple of hours, or help on the stall for the school fête, or give them a lift to collect their car from the garage, are you always ready to say yes? Or would you prefer to get stuck into a good book, or finish the project you're working on, or just put your feet up at the end of the day with your favourite TV programme? Let me tell you, you'll actually get far more out of helping out – maybe not every time, but certainly on balance – because you'll be stepping out of your routine and anything could happen, from an interesting conversation to a huge adventure. That's the thing – you never know what will happen next, especially when you do something different, however mundane it might seem.

Here's something else you can be generous with: knowledge. You must know something that not everyone else does. Surely you could run a session on stop-frame animation at the local youth club, or get a couple of local kids started playing the guitar, or show one of your junior colleagues how to make their Powerpoint presentation stand out, or give a talk about your specialist subject to a local group. You never know, you might even enjoy yourself.

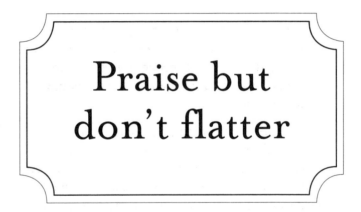

# Praise but don't flatter

People like to be praised, whether it's for a sparkling piece of work or a stylish choice of clothing, a generous gesture or a clever idea. So give them what they want – they'll appreciate you for it.

Praise sometimes get a bad reputation for some reason. Some people misguidedly believe that too much of it is a bad thing, or that it will just sound insincere. If you're worried about this, just remember these guidelines:

- Keep it in proportion. Don't gush all over someone just because their report was neatly laid out. Give them modest recognition, and save the real effusiveness for the really exceptional achievements.

- Don't worry about sounding insincere. The rule is very simple: if it is sincere, it will sound sincere. If you're making it up, it will come across as empty flattery. The thing that needs to change is that you need to voice what you're already thinking more often, not make up things to praise people for.

- Bear in mind that the praise you give says a lot about your values. If you only praise people for being clever, they'll come to assume that that's what matters to you. If you praise people for hard work as well as actual achievement, they'll realise that you care about effort as well as results. Praise people for being generous or hard working or considerate or brave or quick, and those are the things you'll be telling them you care about.

Be loyal

You know your partner can be a bit pushy sometimes. But you don't go round telling that to all and sundry (I hope). Maybe you moan a bit to your best friend or your mum or your brother, but to the outside world you stick up for them, and keep any criticisms to yourself.

Same goes for your best mate. You may be allowed to tell them that they're irresponsible, but you won't admit you think that in front of anyone else. And your boss. No eye for detail? That may be your opinion but you wouldn't share it with the rest of the department.

Am I right? And if not, why not? Look, the point about loyalty is that it isn't about the person you're loyal to – it's about you. Loyalty is an attribute you either have or you don't. You don't turn it on or off according to the merits of the partner or friend or boss in question. That wouldn't be loyalty – that would be expressing an opinion. Loyalty is about you giving your support to someone regardless of your personal view. Whether you agree with them or not. Whether it's easy to stand with them or not. Whether you think it will benefit you or not.

Funny thing is though, it will benefit you. People will recognise loyalty when they see it, and approve no matter what they think about your partner, friend or boss. And they'll realise that if they can get you on their side, they too can rely on your loyalty precisely because you don't switch it on and off as the wind blows. You're an inherently loyal person no matter what.

Don't
talk behind
people's backs

I can remember a colleague I used to have who was fairly popular, being funny and entertaining and very good company. There was a group of about half a dozen of us who worked closely together at one time, and got on very well. One lunchtime he and I went out for a bite to eat together, and he started being quite catty about one of the girls in our group of friends. I really didn't like this at all, and it also set me wondering what he was saying about me behind my back.

You see, it wasn't only the poor girl in question who, if she knew what was going on (and she found out eventually), had reason to feel aggrieved. I wasn't at all sure I wanted to be his friend either. Back then I'd learnt less than I have since, and I carried on hanging out with John for the entertainment value. But I made damn sure I didn't tell him anything private and I never trusted him after that.

No matter how justified your views about people may be, talking behind their backs will always put you in a bad light, and make you appear disloyal. If it isn't necessary to say anything, then it's necessary to say nothing. I'm not saying you can't pass on important information, for the right reasons, to someone who actually needs to know. And of course you and your partner or very best friends are allowed to discuss what you think of people honestly. That's not the same thing at all, as you know. We all know when we're bitching, even when we pretend to ourselves that there's a valid reason for it. But it actually makes us look a lot worse than our intended target.

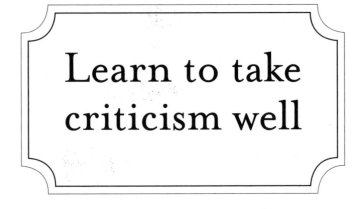

# Learn to take criticism well

I've noticed that the people who can handle criticism best are the most confident ones. They're so sure of their own worth that being told about a minor flaw doesn't cause them immediately to question their whole value and abilities. Tell someone under-confident that they don't always listen very well, and they'll think you're telling them that you don't like them, they're a useless friend, and they should be embarrassed and ashamed every time they deal with anyone. Tell someone self-confident that they don't always listen well, and they'll think, 'Ah, I don't always listen. I should do something about that'.

Of course the people who look confident on the surface aren't necessarily the ones who feel confident underneath. And if you don't feel confident enough to take criticism well, you'll need to fake it. This isn't as bad as it sounds, because after a bit of practice you'll find that, actually, a bit of constructive criticism isn't the end of the world. In fact it's rather helpful. And people will respect you for being able to take it on board.

You've seen people being criticised. Which ones impress you – the ones who get defensive or sulky? Or the ones who say, 'Thanks for the feedback. I'll think about that'? Of course not all feedback is accurate, but if you're known to be able to handle it without getting prickly you can ask others for a second opinion and they'll be happy to give you an honest response.

And look, this is good news. Would you rather everyone knew you had a weak spot but were too nervous of your reaction to say anything to you, or would you prefer to know so that you could sort it out?

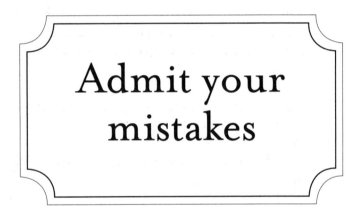

Admit your mistakes

This isn't the same thing as accepting criticism of course, but it's closely related. We all know that everyone makes mistakes, and if you won't admit to them you're not fooling anyone that you've never made any. You may, however, come across as arrogant or pompous or simply unable to recognise when you're wrong.

I'm not advocating some kind of confessional where you go round admitting to everything you can think of, just to appear humble. You don't want to undermine people's confidence in you entirely. But where it's clear something has gone wrong, and it's down to you, then say so. People will respect you more for it.

The same goes for mistakes in the past. If you can tell a story against yourself, admitting you got something wrong, it makes you look human and modest and honest and genuine and self-effacing. All of which are good things.

There is one exception to this approach, mind you. I had a friend years ago who was always late for everything, to the point where it was hugely irritating. I remember her saying to me, 'I'm dreadful at timekeeping, I know, but at least I can admit it'. I thought, 'You mean you know it, you realise the frustration it causes, *and you still do it*? If you were unaware of the hassle I might conceivably forgive you, but if you know what you're doing it's inexcusable'. Once you recognise your mistakes, that doesn't absolve you of any responsibility for correcting them. On the contrary, it makes it imperative.

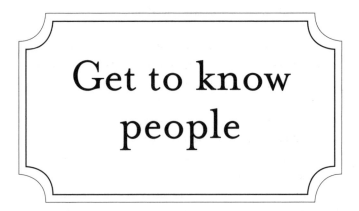

Get to know
people

So you want something – badly. That job, or a bigger house, or a decent holiday, or a calmer outlook on life, or a crucial deal at work, or a decent care package for your ageing father. Whatever it is you need, you're going to struggle to get it without any support. Whether it's at work or at home, from officials or neighbours or your kids' school, you'll find it a whole lot easier with people on your side.

This is always going to be true, before you even know what it is you might want next year or in five years' time. The more of a network you have, the better chance of finding someone to give you the leg-up you need. It's far harder to get what you want if you're a recluse, you know.

So go on, get out there, meet people. Get to know your colleagues – go for the occasional drink after work even if it's not really your thing. Turn up to a residents' meeting or a school parents' do or an event at the sports club. Chat to people, find out more about them, even offer them help if you find someone who could use your support. One day you'll find you need someone who understands cars, or knows a local councillor, or has dealt with a particular customer before, or can tell you how to apply for something, or will nominate you for a committee, or can put you in touch with a good solicitor, or will put a word in with the finance director. And the more people you're on good terms with, the more likely it is you'll know just the person you need.

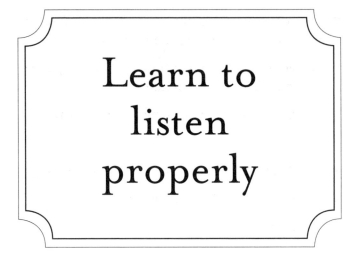

# Learn to listen properly

You'd have thought listening was a pretty basic skill, but how often do you have a conversation with someone where it becomes apparent that you'd both come away from your last discussion on the subject thinking you'd agreed different things? 'But you said *you* were going to pick up the milk on the way home!'. 'No, I said I wouldn't have time, and you said you'd do it...'. Well, all I can say is that at least one of you wasn't listening properly, and quite possibly both. Sometimes it results in drinking black tea for the rest of the evening, and sometimes the consequences are more serious[8].

---

[8] As if messing with your tea wasn't bad enough.

There are lots of things that can stop you listening properly. Recognise any of these?

- You're too busy thinking of what you're going to say as soon as you can get a word in.

- You go off on a different train of thought sparked by something that's been said.

- You know what they're going to say anyway.

- You're bored.

- You don't really understand what they're saying.

- You're distracted by noise or activity.

- You're in a hurry.

If you want to have productive conversations with people – not to mention milk in your tea – you need to recognise when one of these things is happening and stop yourself getting distracted. If necessary you need to say, 'Sorry, I missed that – can you say it again?'. Or, 'I didn't understand that, can you explain it without the jargon?'. Or, 'I can't really concentrate because I'm running late for a meeting. Can we catch up on this properly later?'.

Nobody minds this kind of response, because it shows you want to listen properly. If anything it's flattering – people like to be heard. So train yourself to listen properly and stop pretending.

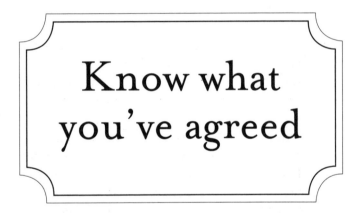

# Know what
# you've agreed

Not every conversation leads to a decision, but often they do. And it's surprising how often everyone has a different recollection of what's been decided. That's why we have minutes for meetings. You might like to try minuting your morning chat with your partner about who's buying the milk, but personally I'd be somewhat irked if you were my partner and you tried to do that at 7.30 am just as I was rushing out the door.

On the other hand, you do need to know who's buying the milk. So you need to get into the habit of at least summarising the conclusion before you go your separate ways. 'Right. So I'll buy the milk and I'll see you back here at about 6.30 then.' This is even more important when you're working towards something you really want. It's crucial you're clear about whether you're calling someone back or waiting for their call. Did your boss ask for your application by this Friday or next Friday? You'll only know if you summarise what's been said, and listen to yourself summarising it (I know that sounds daft, but it is possible to summarise on autopilot and not actually know what you've said – I've done it myself).

If the discussion is at all important, and especially if it's official or work-based in any way, it's also sensible to email your understanding of the decision to the other person – so they can reply if they don't think they heard what you thought they thought they heard (see how easy it is to get confused?). Drop your boss a quick email: 'Thanks for the chat this morning, and I just wanted to confirm that I'll get my application in by next Friday at the latest'.

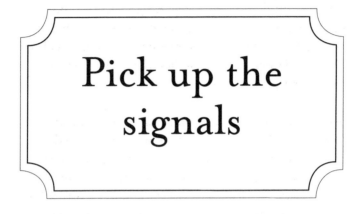

# Pick up the signals

**P**eople don't always say what they're thinking – at least not in words. But that doesn't mean you can't work it out. We say a lot more with our bodies than we do with our mouths, and if you learn to look for the signs you will generally have a pretty good idea of how the other person really feels. Maybe the person you're talking to is silently angry, or nervous, or just plain uninterested but trying to hide it.

Just ignore everything you've been told about some people being intuitive and others just not. Anyone can learn to read body language. In fact, if you're not especially intuitive, you really need to learn how. It's just a matter of training yourself to remember to look for signals.

If you're on the lookout, it's not hard to read body language. And I'll tell you something else – when it conflicts with the words someone is saying, it will be the body language that's telling the truth. You can bet on that.

So what are you looking out for? Well, broadly speaking, relaxed confident people look relaxed and confident. I'm sorry if that sounds too simple, but it really is simple. They sit or stand in a relaxed stance, arms by their sides or in their laps (if they're not holding anything), and they smile readily (and properly, so it reaches their eyes). Tense people (who are angry or anxious or in a hurry, or whatever) are more likely to cross their arms and their legs, fidget, strum their fingers and hold themselves more rigidly. Angry people sound tense, lean forward and often clench their fists. Bored people will look over your shoulder or check their watch – even while telling you they're interested in what you have to say.

The only challenge here is looking for the signs. Reading them is honestly a doddle.

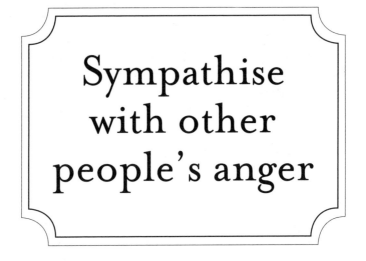

# Sympathise with other people's anger

It's no fun being angry, and it's not something to subject anyone else to if you can help it. But sometimes people are justifiably angry, and sometimes you're in the firing line. If you're at fault, the only thing to do is fess up and apologise, and do what you can to put it right. But what if it isn't your fault? Maybe a customer is angry with your organisation, and you just happen to be the person on the end of the phone or across the counter. Or perhaps your neighbour is livid that your tree surgeon cut down the tree on their side of the fence, when actually you'd never asked them to do any such thing. How are you going to deal with that?

The first thing you're going to do is stay calm. However bad the confrontation, it will get a whole lot worse if you get angry too. What you need to do is recognise *why* people get angry – and that'll be because they don't think they'll get the response they want any other way. So show them they don't need to raise their voice. You can start by listening. If you don't shout back, or incessantly tell them to 'calm down' (which is frankly irritating when you're feeling narked), they'll realise you actually want to hear what they have to say. And they're likely to start calming down pretty fast.

Now you need to sympathise with them. That doesn't mean apologising if it's not your fault – it just means letting them know you understand why they feel angry, and you consider it justified: 'I can see how upsetting that must be'. OK, you're doing well. Deep breath. Now, don't waste their time with long explanations – that's not what they want to hear. Just a quick one-liner will do if it's really essential: 'I certainly never asked them to cut that tree down'.

Nearly there. They should be feeling a lot happier now. But they still want something done, so do whatever you can to help. Give them a refund, or even a gift certificate as well. Offer to replace the tree with a new sapling of their choice. If you can resolve someone's anger effectively enough, you can actually strengthen your relationship with them.

Don't
respond to
tactical anger

OK, everything I just said about dealing with anger – forget it. At least when the anger you're dealing with *isn't* justified. Some people use anger to manipulate, threaten, bully, intimidate or bludgeon you into doing what they want. This is completely different from justified anger, and needs a totally different response. This is toddler-tantrum world, and should be dealt with just as you'd deal with a toddler[9].

In case you don't have children I'll explain the technique (and possibly put you off ever having kids). First you tell them, calmly, that you're not prepared to be shouted at / spoken to like this / abused / bullied / intimidated (delete as applicable), and tell them you'll leave if they don't calm down. Then you carry out the threat if necessary, and leave if they don't stop shouting. If they start up again next time they see you, just keep giving them the same response.

I know this is tough if you're dealing with someone who is – or seems – senior to you. Your boss or your father-in-law or the head of the residents' association. But hey, we're all equal on a human level, and you deserve respect as much as anyone else. What can they do to you? You can't discipline someone for refusing to be cowed by your manipulative intimidation. What actually happens is that these people learn pretty fast that their prima donna tactics don't work on you, and in time they'll stop trying it on because they'll be the ones who look bad when you don't react the way they'd planned.

[9] Although I can't recommend sending your boss, say, to the naughty step.

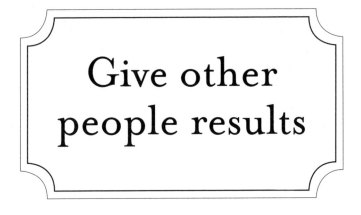

# Give other people results

I once had a PA (yes, I used to be the sort of person who had a PA) who was such a hard worker. She came in on time every day and slogged away until going-home time. Whenever I asked her to do anything, she'd be right there, jotter in hand, taking notes.

I've no idea what she did all day, but she did whatever-it-was very diligently. The reason I don't know what it was she did is that somehow there was never much to show for it. She could place a call for me, or retrieve something from the filing cabinet, but then I could do that for myself. Other than that not a lot seemed to happen unless I was extremely specific about what I wanted and when and how and so on. Then it mostly happened. On a good day.

I have a feeling she organised things constantly. You know, the way you used to organise revision timetables at school – it took so long to get them just right that you never actually had time to do the revision. Trouble was, I actually wanted things to happen. I wanted my car serviced or a difficult customer sorted out or a meeting with four other busy people fixed, or a train ticket to appear magically on my desk the day before I travelled. Nope. None of that.

The filing system was immaculate though.

Your boss wants results. Targets met – or preferably exceeded. Your partner wants that holiday booked, or the lawn mower serviced. Your kids want the cinema tickets arranged. The May Fair committee wants the white elephant stall organised. People want things to happen. Not just to sound keen and look good, but actually to happen. You know what you have to do. Do it.

Be part
of your
organisation

You're part of a team. The family, the company, the council – I don't know what teams you belong to but you certainly should. The word team may not be the one that springs to mind when I mention some of those things, but it should be. You need to view any cohesive group you belong to as a team. This comes more naturally to some people than others, but you can learn to do it.

The rest of the group all like a team player. So do you, when it comes to the other people involved. You'll be far better regarded if people can see that you're one of them. Because what's the alternative? To see the group as a separate entity, to refer to the company or the committee as 'them' rather than 'us'. People notice these things, you know. If you're not part of the team, not talking about 'we', not identifying with its successes – and its failures – you're distancing yourself from it. That's not very friendly is it? Nor is it very loyal.

This is important but usually easy with your family. Hopefully you've always felt like one of the clan. It can be more of a challenge at work though, and with other 'official' commitments. But that's where it matters most. If you want to get the best out of other people, and get them on your side, it's crucial that you don't give the impression that there's more than one side to be on. If you're all pulling together, all part of the same gang, they'll appreciate your input and want to give you all the support you need.

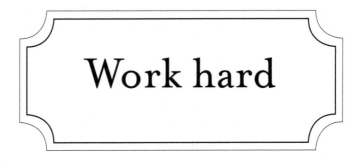
Work hard

There's no substitute.

People want to help those who help themselves by working hard. If you want support you need to show that you're making most of the running yourself. No one's going to work hard on your behalf if they can see you twiddling your thumbs.

I'm not telling you to labour 24 hours a day without respite. You need to do other things as well as work. Rest and play, obviously – everyone knows that. But you should put in plenty of working hours, and when your time is allocated to work, that's precisely what you do.

Listen, no one owes you anything. We get what we want by a combination of a bit of luck and a lot of hard work. If you want stuff, you work. You slog. You graft. Simple as that.

Work right

Hard work is crucial, but it has to be the right kind of hard work. No, I can't tell you what that is because it's different for everyone. I can tell you that there's no point organising your revision timetable when you should actually be revising. And many's the hard worker who feels aggrieved at not being promoted because they put in more hours than anyone else on the team (but didn't actually meet their targets).

If you want things, you need to make sure that you're investing your energy in the right direction. It's not about effort in, but about results out. How you spend your working time should be determined by the results you need to achieve. If you can achieve those results without trying, you've set your targets too low. Remember, people must see you working as hard as they do or they won't want to work even harder to help you when it's needed.

So work out what you need to do to get what you want – the evening classes you need to attend, the sales you need to achieve, the bills you need to pay off, the qualifications you need to gain, the weight you need to lose. Then think about exactly where you need to put the effort in to make it actually happen. What will be crucial? That's where you need to invest all that hard work.

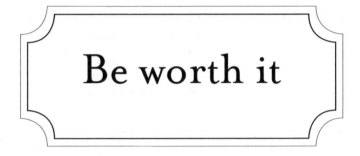

# Be worth it

There are lots of things you might want – lots of reasons you may have picked up this book – and many of them have nothing to do with work. A lot of them do though, and of those the most frequent ambitions people tell me about are getting pay rises and promotions. Indeed, even if it's not top of your own personal list, you probably wouldn't say no if a raise or promotion was in the offing.

I'll tell you where most people go wrong, too. There's a kind of assumption that if you're doing a good job and you've been there a long time, you somehow deserve it. Wrong. Listen, times are hard.

Your boss can't give you an upgrade of any kind without a damn good reason. So you'd better give them one.

This is a perfect example of not only working hard but also working at the right things. You are only going to get that raise or promotion if you can demonstrate that you are giving your company more value than they expected when you started the job, or last had a raise. That means you have to show them how you're doing one of these things:

- You are exceeding the targets you were set.

- You are earning, or saving, the organisation significantly more money than they expected.

- You are more valuable because you've gained qualifications or experience.

- You have additional responsibilities that weren't in your remit before.

- You give as much (or greater) value than other employees who earn more than you.

That's what gives your boss the excuse to increase your recognition from the company. Hard work on its own is no more than you were originally contracted to provide. But demonstrating increased value gives you a really strong case.

**PART 3**

# Help them
# to say yes

The more you can help someone say yes to you, the less you actually have to ask for what you want, in so many words. You know yourself that some people are easy to say yes to, for all sorts of reasons. Maybe the request is straightforward, maybe it doesn't require much effort from you, perhaps they've asked at just the right moment, or in a particularly charming way, or maybe you owe them a favour, or perhaps you just like them and want to help.

Whether you feel comfortable asking directly or whether you want to find an indirect way to get what you want, the easier you can make it for the other person to help you, the more likely you are to get what you want. And the key to all that is to put yourself in their shoes and see it from their perspective. So that's what we'll do next.

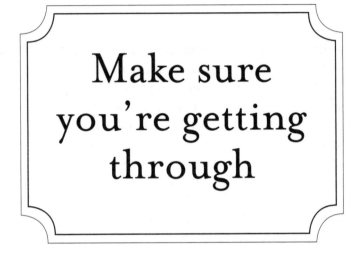

# Make sure you're getting through

No one is going to give you what you want if they don't know what it is – not on purpose anyway. And some people just don't listen properly. You may be asking for something big from them, or they may just be giving you a bit of help along the way, but either way you need to make sure they've taken on board what it is you need.

You know the people in your life who never listen properly, and then like as not blame you for the communication problem: 'You never said...'. Right. We're going to make absolutely sure they hear this time. So the first thing to do is to work out exactly what you want to say, and find the most succinct way you can of expressing it. Practise it if need be, so you'll get it right. 'I'm looking for cover on Thursday afternoon. Are you free?'

If there's any complication repeat it in different words, maybe even ask them to say it back to you, 'just so I know I'm making sense'. (Just be careful not to do it in a way that gets their back up or belittles them – you really have to judge this in the situation, I can't actually be there with you.) This can help to fix it in their mind. Then summarise again at the end of the conversation.

If you feel the other person doesn't fully grasp that you have a problem that needs solving, ask them questions: 'How would *you* go about getting the customer to agree to a delayed delivery date? Bearing in mind that they have clients shouting at them already…'.

Listen, if it's that important to you that you free up this time, or get onto this course, or meet this deadline, or achieve that target, you can't overestimate the importance of getting the right information through to the people you need on your side.

And make
sure *they're*
getting
through to you

So that last point was about people who don't listen properly. But what about the people who don't express themselves clearly? If you need information or help from them you need to be able to hear what they're telling you.

I had a colleague who spoke in a very strong, categorical way, with a forceful personality. (That doesn't sound very amiable but actually she was – very sparky and self-assured.) Anyway, after I'd been working with her a while I noticed that I wasn't always clear about what she'd been talking about. I obviously hadn't been concentrating properly. I must try harder. A week or two later I came away from another discussion with her… only to realise I hadn't actually grasped what she wanted from me.
I smacked myself over the wrist again and, apologising for my vagueness, mentioned it to someone else, who said, 'Do you know, I thought it was me. I have the same problem'. In fact, although her manner seemed clear, it had been masking her serious inability to express herself in black and white.

The way to overcome this is to ask questions – specifically closed questions that invite yes, no, or one-word answers: 'Will you be here for Tuesday's meeting?', 'Can we be confident of selling more than 2,000 of these in the first month?' or 'Are you happy to babysit for me if I babysit for you?'. Don't stop until you're sure you have the information you want.

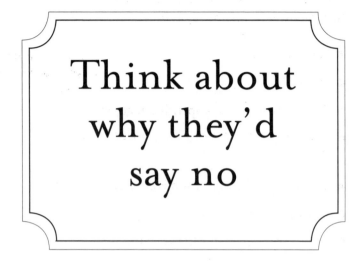

# Think about why they'd say no

Now, we know that some people find it easier to say no than others, but almost everyone would prefer to say yes if they can. Not at any cost of course, but why not be helpful when you can? Even the most cynical people can see the advantage in being owed a favour. So if they say no, there will be a reason for it. Some people will say no for a minor reason, others will help if they conceivably can, but there's always a reason why they might say no.

So what's it likely to be? If you can second guess their objections, you can put yourself into a much better position. So think through the reasons why they might be going to say no:

● It's a lot of work.

● It will cost them.

● It will give you a competitive edge over them.

● They'll never get it past their boss / partner / friend.

● It entails dealing with someone difficult.

● They haven't got time.

● It will show up a weakness or mistake of theirs.

● It will be cold / uncomfortable / dirty / messy.

That's not an exhaustive list, but it's a start. Sometimes the reason might be that they don't like / trust / feel confident in you, but we've already made sure that won't be the case so I've left it off the list. You're much better placed than me to work out their objection, and for goodness sake don't forget that there may be more than one objection, and you need to think of them all. That way you can start preparing the ground.

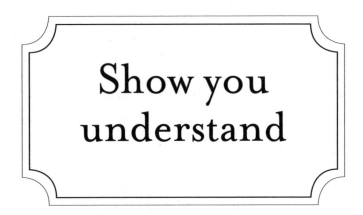

Show you
understand

Your job now is to make sure you let the other person know that you have grasped the problems involved. Not just their own, but the things in the system that might conflict with what you want. Let them see that you understand why their partner might not agree, or that you know what extra paperwork it will entail, or that you realise what the knock-on effects will be for the membership.

Once people see that you really understand the issues, they're much more likely to listen to you. Stands to reason. Why would they take you seriously if you clearly haven't a clue what's going on, or are ignorant of the facts, or haven't got to grips with the prevailing mood among the workforce? If, on the other hand, you're thoroughly versed in the nuances and subtleties of the situation, then your opinion is going to be worth having, and your advice on how to play things will be valuable.

It's never enough just to work out for yourself the complications or ramifications or subtext. You have to think them through, and then make sure the other person knows that you know. It will give your case far more authority.

# Be objective

Your credibility is vital. No one is going to come round to your way of thinking if they don't trust your judgement. They won't agree to drop the asking price, or bring forward the launch date, or invest in a new sports hall, or send you on a training course, just because you want it. They need to believe that it's actually the right thing to do.

This means that you must avoid giving subjective judgements. Don't say something is 'great' or 'best'. Be specific about it: it's the most accurate this or the cheapest that or the fastest something or other. And it's not 'incredibly fast', it's 'capable of speeds up to 95mph'. These are objective measures, that you should be able to back up. They're not just your opinion. That gives them clout.

So when you approach someone to talk about giving you what you want, make sure you have with you all the data you could need to back up these objective claims of yours. Don't wait to be asked. Show you've done your research and volunteer the results. Demonstrate clearly why the asking price is too high, or sales will benefit from a March launch, or schools with modern sports halls are more successful than those without[10], or how people with this training can contribute to their organisations.

Now you look like a real expert on the subject, instead of someone with a personal motive.

[10] Yes I made that up (so it's not objective or backed up with hard data).

# Give them an excuse to make an exception

Sometimes you need someone to give you something that goes against their normal actions, or risks undermining a principle of theirs, or may set a precedent they wouldn't want set. When this happens you need to help them find an excuse to say yes to you and still say no at other times that suit them. They might be able to come up with their own excuse of course, but why bother? For them it's as easy to say no. You're the one with the vested interest here, so you'd better do the hard work.

Maybe your mum feels that if she comes on holiday with you to help with the kids she'll have to do the same for both your siblings, and that's too much of a commitment. Perhaps the management board have already stipulated that they won't take on any new staff. You need to help them change their minds – and what they need is an excuse for making an exception in this case.

Try telling your mum, 'I realise it's a lot of your time, and we could always cope fine when we had two children, same as Jack and Rachel cope with theirs. But now we have the twins as well it's more than double the work…'. There's a justification she can use if Jack or Rachel asks why she doesn't come on their holidays as an unpaid babysitter.

When it comes to your proposal to the board, explain that you agree staffing levels should be kept to a minimum. But this case is different. Two extra, experienced staff to work with the new software will free up four people to sell full time, so the increase will pay for itself in the first three months.

If you can think of a reason for making you the exception to the rule, and one that they can then use on anybody else who asks for the same thing, you're in the best possible place for them to say yes to you.

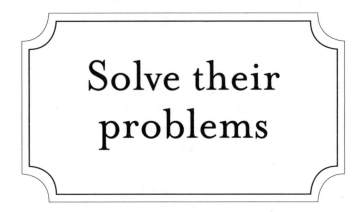

Solve their
problems

So now you've worked out what might stop them saying yes, you need to come up with a plan to counteract their objection. This isn't difficult, although you might need to get creative.

Suppose your neighbour might say no to babysitting regularly so you can go to an evening class. What's her reason, do you reckon? She doesn't want to commit that much time? Well, how about you offer to do something for her to compensate – if you mowed her lawn every weekend she'd get back the time she gave you. Or you could promise to have the kids in bed before she arrives so she can use the time to get on with her own stuff.

Why would your boss say no to sending you on a particular course? Maybe she can't justify the cost in the current economic climate. Or perhaps she'd have to clear it with *her* boss, and she knows that will be a pain. So you need to work out how the company will get its money back through the increase in your value. And perhaps for good measure you should put together a well-researched written report on the benefits, so your boss can pass it straight on to her manager. Then it's down to your powers of persuasion and she doesn't have to argue the case herself.

Getting the picture? Listen, if you want this thing enough you can be creative about removing the other person's objections to helping you. Then how are they going to be able to say no?

# Read the clues

S ome people will give you an unequivocal answer straight off. But some people won't. Maybe they don't want to seem rude, or perhaps they really want to help but can't, or maybe they're still undecided. Then again, you may well not actually have asked in so many words, so they don't feel they have to give an answer.

That doesn't mean that they don't drop clues though. Hints even. And you need to listen for them. Especially if you're trying to get what you want without actually having to ask. And there are plenty of clues to listen out for. Let me give you a few examples so you can see what I'm driving at:

- 'Hmmm. I wonder whether Ali might be able to help you...' tells you that this person wants to help, and might be prepared to approach Ali on your behalf.

- 'I don't know if I can manage a Thursday...' tells you that if you can change the night, they may be able to help.

- 'It's going to be tricky persuading the finance director...' means that this person is probably on your side but you need to furnish them with convincing figures.

- 'I've been meaning to do something about shedding a bit of weight myself...' indicates that this person might join you on your diet – which may give you a better chance of success.

Once you have the clues you can get on with finding ways to remove the obstacles that might stop you getting what you're after.

Learn what gets them going

I had a boss once who was convinced that anyone would do whatever you wanted if you offered them enough money. Anytime anyone needed motivating he'd tempt them with the possibility of a pay rise, or the promise of an additional bonus, or the suggestion of a promotion. Funny thing was, there were only a couple of people on his team who ever worked harder for all his attempts to motivate them. He couldn't understand it. What's more, there were plenty of unmotivated staff moaning that they never got any thanks for all their hard work.

Not everyone is motivated by money. Sure, if it makes no odds we'd all rather have more of it please, even if not for ourselves. But that doesn't mean it's what really drives us, what excites us, what makes us feel good, what makes all the effort worthwhile. People are motivated by all kinds of different things. Think about your kids if you have them, or your best friends. Most of them want status more than money, or we want recognition, or power, or responsibility, or job satisfaction, or challenge, or just a simple thank you.

Once you've identified what drives people that's when you can really start to get what you want, by making sure you trade it for what they really want.

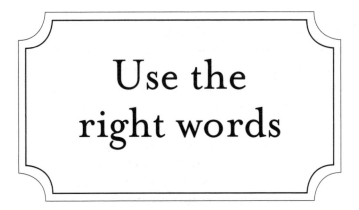

# Use the
# right words

It's important, if you want someone to say yes, that you talk about what you want – whether you're actually asking or not – in terms that will make it sound appealing. And they may not be attracted by the same things as you. In the same way that you need to know what drives people, you also need to know which words give them a positive feeling – and which don't.

If you were trying to describe a fairground ghost train ride to a typical teenage boy, you might tell them, 'Come on – you'll love it! It's really fast and scary!'. That would do the trick with a lot of teenagers I know. But it certainly wouldn't work on some of their grandparents. You'd need to tell them, 'It's completely safe, and it's so naff it's funny'. Same ride, different words.

When you get to know people well – your boss or your family or your kids or your friends – you discover that they all have words that turn them on or off. Some people are a sucker for anything 'exciting', or 'funny', or 'quirky'. I used to have a manager who would agree to anything so long as she was convinced it was 'reliable' or 'proven'. She liked words that sounded safe. It's always worth listening to the kind of language they use themselves – that can give you clues as to what kind of words will work best on them.

If you want someone to support you work out which words they like to hear, and then use those words to convince them to do it.

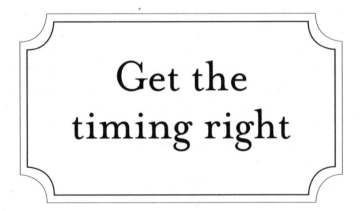

Get the
timing right

Getting what you want can be a long-term plan. I know someone who has just spent five years restoring a classic boat, while living on it in the cold and wet, and now finally (and deservedly) has a fabulous and comfortable home that is, at last, sufficiently watertight to float. He knew from the start that what he wanted would take five years, and it did. You may have some minor wants that can be satisfied quickly and easily, but most of the big plans and dreams take longer.

So you know well in advance that you're going to need things from other people. When you think through how you're going to go about achieving this, think about when you're going to approach them. Your partner may always go through a period of stress at a particular time of year when several contracts come up for renewal – so that's not going to be the best time to ask for extra support.

Similarly, don't approach your boss for a pay rise the month after a salary review, or when the last quarter's figures have just come in and are particularly depressing – even if you're the only one keeping them afloat. Much better to ask in the days or weeks after you clinch a lucrative deal.

You make it far easier for people to support you if you approach them when the time suits *them*, and not just you. So consider things from their perspective, and fit your schedule around them as far as you can.

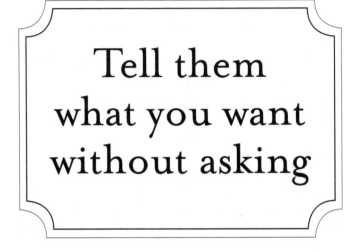

# Tell them what you want without asking

OK, I said on the cover of this book that you could get what you wanted without having to ask. And you can – perhaps not always but most of the time. However, if you need someone else to give it to you, you may need to let them know that you want it. Without asking.

The simplest way to do this, blindingly obvious as it is, is just to *say* that you want it. No asking. So you can let your boss know at your appraisal that you see yourself moving up the career ladder swiftly, or that you see yourself working ultimately on the PR side of marketing. Next time an opportunity arises for a promotion or new responsibilities, they'll know you're interested already. So if they think you're in with a chance they'll come to you.

You can similarly let your friends and out-of-work colleagues know what your aims are. When someone else gets invited to join the board of trustees of the local charity you support, you can say, 'Good for them. I'd love to do that'. Someone listening who might not have considered you may well make a mental note for next time.

Let your mum know about your friend who always takes her sister on holiday to help with the kids. Tell her, 'I think that's such a good idea. It must be a huge help to have an extra adult there'. Maybe she'll offer before you need to ask.

If someone's in a position to help you, and they'd like to support you, why wouldn't they offer? I'll tell you why: because they have no idea that you want it. Apparently one survey of single people found that 98 per cent of respondents would like their friends to help find them a new partner, but four out of five had never actually let their friends know this. Daft or what?

# Don't keep dropping hints

Letting people know what you want (without asking) is a really sensible strategy. But while saying outright 'I'd like that' or 'What a great idea, I could do with one of those' is a sensible approach, it's not a good idea to keep dropping not-so-subtle hints.

I had an aunt who used to do this. 'Oh, if only I could spend Christmas with family. It must be so lovely.' 'You're so lucky to have such nice friends. No one ever asks me to dinner.' The fact is that this used to irritate us all so much that we deliberately ignored the hints. They had a whingy, emotional blackmail quality about them that we just refused to be sucked in by. If she'd just asked straight, 'Can I come for Christmas?', we'd probably have said yes. Or indeed if she'd let us know she'd like to come and then shut up about it.

No one wants to be pestered, especially in an indirect manner. So if you're going for the 'don't ask, just let them know what you want' approach, you need to say it once and then let it alone. Maybe – if you're not sure they got the message – you can mention it again a few months later, or you can mention it in front of somebody else. That's it. It's a very useful approach if you don't want to ask (and sometimes even if you don't mind asking) but it's not one you can overuse and get away with it.

Listen, the last thing you want to do is irritate your potential benefactor. So make sure you're being straight about letting them know what you want, and then letting it drop. Avoid, at all costs, the manipulative hint-dropping thing because you'll just alienate people that way.

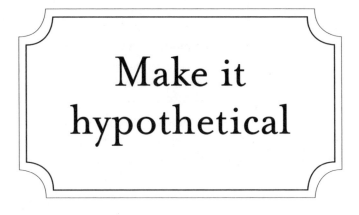

# Make it hypothetical

A variation on letting them know what you want is to express what you want hypothetically. This is no more (or less) likely to achieve the aim. The point is that it's a direct, straightforward and honest way of asking, which you might find easier than actually asking. It comes across as being far less pushy – because it doesn't require the other person to give you a yes or no answer – so if you are remotely under-assertive it may appeal to you. Here's how it goes:

- 'If ever you were thinking of selling that piece of land, I might be interested.'

- 'If a job came up in the PR department, I'd really love the opportunity to apply for it.'

- 'If you need another trustee on the board in future, I'd love to be more involved.'

If you're feeling very brave you can turn it around and request a hypothetical answer:

- 'If I could find an evening class to learn another language, do you think you might be able to babysit one night a week?'

- 'If we find the perfect house and it's just a bit over our budget, is there any chance you and mum might be able to help us meet the difference?'

- 'If Sian does transfer to the Manchester branch, could I be considered as her replacement?'

This version does require some kind of response, but you're very much sounding the other person out rather than asking directly. And it will give you a lot of useful information to help towards getting what you want.

Ask questions

Here's another way to ask without actually having to ask. You simply ask the other person what they'd do in your position. How would they achieve the thing you're after? It's quite likely that they'll realise that your best bet is to get them to help and, if you've laid the groundwork making yourself someone they'd like to say yes to, there's a good chance they'll offer.

So you could ask your boss how they'd go about getting into PR if they were in your position. How would they achieve it? Or tell your mum you find holidays so exhausting with four kids that you're not sure you can face going away. What should you do?

Be careful not to sound as if you're deliberately manipulating them into offering to help. That will irritate them and thus deter them. You really are asking for advice, because if they suggest something you haven't thought of, that could genuinely be helpful even if it doesn't entail them offering practical help themselves.

# Ask for advice instead of a job

Here's a very canny technique for getting a job in a new organisation, or a first job, or a position in a voluntary sector organisation. As a matter of fact, this very strategy got me my first proper job.

Suppose you want to work in a particular field that's new to you, or in a certain organisation, and you want to meet the person who could give you that job. The fact is that if you write or email and ask to go and see someone because you want them to give you work, they'll almost certainly say no. No one likes to turn down a job applicant, and it's easier to turn down the initial request for a meeting.

So you don't ask for a job. In fact, you specify that you're *not* asking for a job. You say something along the lines of, 'I realise you don't have any vacancies at the moment, but I'd hugely appreciate your advice on how to get into the industry / organisation'. Of course you then explain why you want to work in that field so much, and why you want *their* advice in particular.

Few people can resist flattery, especially when it's sincere. And without the pressure of having to turn you down, most people will agree to meet so you can pick their brains. Actually, however, if they decide that you've got all the passion and brains and commitment and knowledge and expertise they want, why wouldn't they offer you a job? If not now, then as soon as they have a suitable vacancy? Or they'd recommend someone else to approach, and put in a word or let you use their name. If they like you and think you have what it takes, they'll want to help you and they'll have the power to do it.

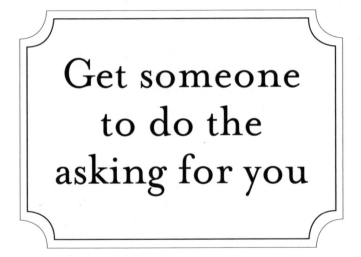

Get someone
to do the
asking for you

I f you don't want to have to ask, why not get someone else to do it for you? No this won't always work, but it often can. Either you get them to ask directly, or you get them to sound out the other person so you know their likely response. It'll be much easier to go on and ask for yourself if you already know they're going to say yes.

Thank you, yes, I have noticed the deliberate mistake. You'll still have to ask the person who's doing the asking. I do realise that. Which is why this tactic is for those occasions when it's easy to ask the go-between. I'm assuming you can ask some people to do some things – it's just the big stuff you struggle with. Presumably you can ask the dog to sit, or ask your partner to pass the milk, or your kids to put on their shoes. So you need to get someone you *can* ask to do the bit that you don't feel comfortable with[11].

Maybe your sister can talk to your mum about going on holiday with you so you can have a bit more of a rest from the kids. Perhaps your line manager can ask their boss if you'd be able to work from home a couple of days a week. Maybe your best mate *can* ask that girl you like whether she'd go on a date with you?

This approach has an added advantage in that it implies the go-between is on your side. Why else would they ask for you? And the other person is more likely to give the matter serious thought if you've got support.

[11] So don't ask your kids to see if your boss will give you a pay rise, or the dog to sound out the bank manager about a loan.

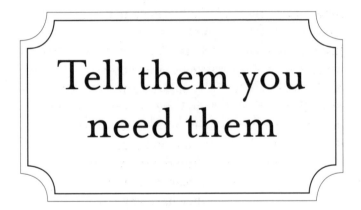

Tell them you
need them

O oh but people do like to be flattered. I've said it before. And I'll repeat that any flattery must be sincere. Lots of people respond remarkably well to feeling needed, and if it's true the flattery isn't hollow.

If you need someone, why not say so? It will give them a warm feeling, and help them to realise that if they don't help you, the job of supporting you won't just be passed on to the next person because there isn't a next person. You're relying on *them*. That should focus their mind a bit. Help them to say yes.

Just one thing here – this is another of those times when you have to be sure not to emotionally blackmail the other person. You're not trying to make them feel guilty about you – you just want them to know that they're important to your plans. If you tip over into implying that if they don't help you all your hopes and dreams will be cruelly dashed, that's emotional blackmail and they won't like it. What's more, if they have any sense, they won't help you.

The clue to the difference is in the word 'emotional'. If you tell them matter-of-factly that you need their help, and then don't bang on about it, you're fine. If you allow emotion into the proceedings – being whiny or simpering or pathetic or telling them how if they don't help you'll suffer this or that – that's when you've gone too far. Especially if you keep going on about it.

# Don't rush them

I had a boss once who had a great line for preventing people pressuring him. If ever you tried to push him into a decision about anything he'd say, 'If you want an answer now, it's no'. That was really helpful, actually, brusque as it sounded, because he could easily have just said no without letting on that you might have got a yes if you'd waited. That's what lots of people do, sometimes without really recognising that they're doing it.

The fact is that, for most decisions, no is a safer answer than yes. It simply maintains the status quo – how much trouble can you create just by declining someone's request? Very little. Whereas saying yes could lead to all sorts of hassle and ramifications and difficulties and unpleasantness. You really can't afford to say yes unless you've had plenty of time to think through all the possible consequences. And if you're not being given that time – if you're being put under pressure for an answer – it's much safer to say no. Not to mention quicker and easier and gets the whole thing off your back.

So if you want to help the other person say yes to you, it's really important not to rush them into a decision. If they're really dragging their feet to the point where it's causing problems, try asking them when they'll be able to give you an answer. That doesn't pressure them but lets you know where you stand.

As a complete aside here, I would just remark that this is a brilliant answer to give other people when you don't want them rushing you. I find it works very well with kids, who try to catch you in an unguarded moment to ask for things you're not sure they should have. Try saying 'If you want an answer now, it's no' to a teenager, and suddenly they're happy for you to take all the time you need to think about it.

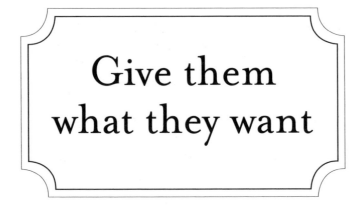

# Give them what they want

It would be lovely if everyone in this world was filled with altruism and love of humankind. Well, some of them are of course, but even they still have personal wants too. So give them something in exchange for saying yes.

I don't mean a bunch of flowers or a box of chocolates – although there are times when that may be appropriate. I mean *before* they've said yes. Let them know that helping you will benefit them in some way.

No, I'm not talking about blackmail. I'm not suggesting you slip your boss a brown envelope full of used tenners in exchange for putting your name forward to head up the next big project. Indeed I'm not talking about making anything conditional on them saying yes. I'm just saying you should draw their attention to any benefits they'll derive personally from saying yes to you.

If your dad minds the kids for you he'll get more time with them, followed by a peaceful evening once they've gone to bed. If the next PR manager comes from your boss's department that will reflect well on the boss. If your partner helps you lose weight you're much more likely to agree to the kind of holiday that entails lazing around in a swimsuit. If your in-laws help you buy a house you'll be able to move nearer to them[12].

Sometimes you can add in a benefit (we can move nearer to you), and sometimes it's just a matter of drawing their attention to a benefit that will come automatically if you get what you want. Either way, make sure they're fully aware of all the ways this could help them get something they want too.

---

[12] Or further away – I don't know how you and your in-laws feel about each other.

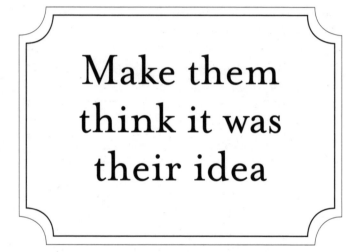

Make them
think it was
their idea

If you're anything like me, it goes against the grain to give anyone else the credit for your good ideas. But look, who gets credit isn't the point here. The real prize is the whatever-you-want that you're reading this book to help you get. Who cares about little bits of credit along the way? And in fact, following on from the previous page, if the other person thinks there's credit to be had for a good idea, let them have it. It all helps you on your way.

All you have to do is follow the logical steps towards the idea without actually reaching the conclusion. Then you just wait for them to finish your sentence for you. 'Of course it would be lovely to live nearer to you, but houses round your way are that bit pricier. I don't think we'd be able to run to a fourth bedroom and we really do need it. We're just a few thousand short for a deposit. We'll have to wait a few years for our next move before we can just pop down the road to see each other.' To which, hopefully, your mum replies, 'Unless… maybe we could lend you just a few thousand… it would be lovely to have you close by…', and you respond, 'What a clever idea!'. Now it's her idea and not yours it's much harder for her to change her mind.

Sometimes, if they're almost there but not getting it, you can wait until the conversation moves on – maybe wait a week or two – and then say, 'Do you know, I thought your idea about expanding our remit / moving house / joining forces was a clever / sensible / workable one'. If you're praising the idea they're unlikely to deny it, and maybe they misremembered – maybe it was their idea…

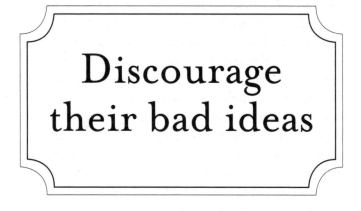

# Discourage their bad ideas

Of course, you're not the only one with ideas. Other people will come up with schemes and suggestions too. Some of them will be good, some may even be directly helpful to you, and some... well, some will just be downright bad ideas. And, what's more, they may threaten to get in the way of what you want. Like your partner's suggestion of moving your in-laws in with you. It might work for some people but in your case it's clearly going to be a disaster. Or your colleague proposing that you all take it in turns to project manage the year's trade shows instead of having one overall PM. Or your best friend insisting that you really must join her on her latest fad diet.

I know one couple who have been together many years. He is somewhat prone to coming up with suggestions that she really can't countenance. However, if she says so it can start an argument and he may become more entrenched. This is the danger when you disagree with someone – you draw attention to their idea and encourage them to promote it more actively, which is the opposite of what you want. So in the case of this particular couple (and probably many others) she's developed a very successful technique over the years. When he comes up with an idea she doesn't like, she just says, 'Mmmm'. Faced with this resounding lack of enthusiasm, but without a direct challenge, he generally forgets about it sooner or later.

So don't try to shout down the ideas that get in your way. Just ignore them and there's a good chance they'll simply go away.

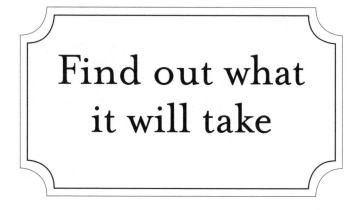

# Find out what it will take

Here's a genius of a technique for getting any kind of work-related upgrade – promotion, pay rise, extra perks – and it can work for other things too such as getting a loan from your bank manager. It takes a bit of patience, but you'll get what you want in the end. And we all know that if it's worth having, it's worth waiting for.

If your boss has turned down your request – or if you don't want to ask or don't feel there'd be any point right now – you ask this killer question: 'What would I have to do to be worth a pay rise (or whatever) in six months' time?'.

If you think about it, they can't very well say 'nothing'. They'd be telling you that you can't add any more value to the organisation. So they don't want you to work harder or improve your results? Of course they do.

That means they have to give you an answer. And whatever that answer is, that's your target. If you can achieve that in six months' time, they'll have to give you a pay rise. Especially if you've followed up this conversation with an email confirming what's been said.

Obviously it doesn't have to be six months – you can ask whatever you think will be appropriate in terms of timing. But it is important that your boss is specific. It's no good just saying you'd need to 'increase sales' or 'get more qualifications'. Increase sales to what level? Which qualifications? It needs to be specific, so they can't argue with you when you do it.

If your boss tries to waffle and say they don't know exactly, money's tight and they're not sure what senior management would feel, ask them to find out for you. And email them little reminders if necessary until they do. Remember you're not asking for a handout. You're asking at what point would your value to the company be so great that it would be profitable to pay you more to incentivise you.

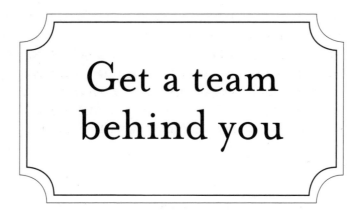

Get a team
behind you

If you want someone to do something big for you, which will take time or money or commitment or hassle or effort, they will probably want to take advice or consult other people. Management will want everyone's views on whether to open that new branch (the one that you want to run). Your parents will seek your brother and sister's opinion on whether to move to a smaller house nearer to yours. That man you've taken a strong fancy to might want to see what his friends think before he asks you on a date.

So it's only logical to get as many people as you can onside before you ask the key person. That way, the advice they'll get when they start consulting will be in your favour. If everyone in the meeting is arguing in favour of the new branch, the management are far more likely to agree. Mum and dad will be much more inclined to make the move if all their children support it.

So prime all these people, and convince them of your case. If this is a big deal, treat each one as a challenge in itself, and use all the strategies we've covered to get them to support you. It will take time, maybe – effort, certainly – but boy will it be worth it when just about everyone comes out in your favour.

PART 4

And if you
really *do* have
to ask…

OK I lied. At least, I didn't exactly lie. I said I'd tell you how to get what you want without having to ask, and I have. I just omitted to mention that occasionally there is nothing for it but to ask directly. So to make up for misleading you slightly, I'm now including a few guidelines so that when you *do* have to ask, it can be as painless and as effective as possible.

Ideally you can practise these techniques as much as possible until you find that, actually, asking's not so bad. After all, it can be the simplest and most straightforward way to get what you want. That doesn't mean that all the rest of this book is wasted, because you'll still need to use most of the skills and tactics and techniques and strategies and ploys we've covered. But being able to just plain ask will certainly add another string to your bow.

So here we have it.

How to get what you want without having to ask *twice*.

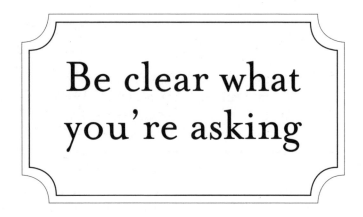

Be clear what
you're asking

Sure, some requests are pretty straightforward. Can I have Friday off to travel to a family wedding? Can I extend my overdraft? Will you go out with me? But often there's a more complicated agenda. Suppose you want your partner to help you lose weight, and you're asking them to support you. How? You want them to tell you off every time you look at the biscuit tin? Agree to stop cooking certain foods? Go on the diet with you? You need to know what you're asking, or how will they know whether to say yes?

Here's another example. You want your boss to give you more responsibility. So you ask them. And they say, what extra responsibilities do you want? When do you want to start? Will you need extra support? Are you prepared to put in longer hours? And if the answer is no, is that it, or are you going to ask them to reconsider if you enrol on an evening course to brush up your skills, or get more experience over the next few months, or wait until someone in the department moves on?

Don't go into the conversation until you've thought through all the possibilities, and are clear in your mind about exactly what it is you're asking. Because if you don't know, they're certainly not going to. And if they're not sure exactly what they're agreeing to, well… it's easier just to say no.

Pick your
moment

L ast night I was busy trying to cook for the family. The oil had run out so the range cooker[13] wasn't working, and I had to use the faffy little emergency electric cooker that never cooperates fully. I'd had to work late (writing this book) so I was quite tight for time. In any spare moment I could grab I was putting together my youngest son's lunchbox for the morning and changing the laundry round. I was also trying to get a pill down a recalcitrant cat, which was the moment my eldest son decided to ask me if he could cook some cakes. Guess what I told him? (But please leave out the language I used under my breath.)

If you want someone to say yes to you, the time to ask them is when they're feeling chilled, happy, relaxed, full of the joys of the world, at one with the universe. If you can't catch them in that mood, at least wait until they're cheerful and not in a hurry. Finding the right moment can seem like a minor detail, but getting it wrong is actually one of the biggest reasons people say no.

[13] Yes, I'm the sort of person who has a range cooker. And a cat asleep in front of it (except when it's cold because the oil has run out).

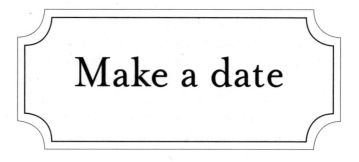

Make a date

Sometimes you know that you'll get what you want if you catch someone in the right mood. And this may be only a small (though important) step towards your final goal. Catching the right moment works for certain people, but others are always busy, and you tend to feel you haven't got their full attention. Or this is a vital stage in your plan, even the crucial point, and it's really important you discuss what you want in detail. Maybe you need to convince your partner that now is the time to start a family, or to persuade your boss to interview you for the new post.

In that case it's really essential you have their full attention for several minutes at least. It's just not going to work if they have to dash off before you're done asking. So the answer is obvious: make an appointment. Don't just aim to catch your boss on a quiet day – ask for an appointment. If they want to know why, say you want to talk about your work, or your performance.

In the case of your partner, if home life gets busy you can arrange to go out for a walk or a meal in order to get them alone for a decent length of time. You can invite a neighbour or friend over for tea or out for a drink. Whether it's a formal meeting or an informal get-together, what you need to organise is time away from other distractions so you can concentrate on what you're going to ask.

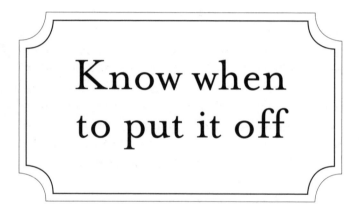

Know when
to put it off

This is something you really want, something important to you. Even so, it just occasionally happens that you realise before you get to your meeting that you're not actually properly prepared for it. Maybe you were going to prepare and then some crisis got in the way. Or perhaps you only discovered some vital fact at the last minute.

Whatever the reason, you're now supposed to be meeting your boss, your child's head teacher, your mother, your bank manager, your neighbour – whoever – in a few hours, and you realise you're not ready. They may ask questions or raise arguments that you have no good answer to. What do you do?

You postpone, that's what. Rearrange the meeting or ask them if you can have that chat next week instead. I know, I know, you don't want to mess people around, and you don't want to wait. But what else can you do? You only get one chance at a first approach – and it's always so much harder to have to go back and re-propose whatever it is, because you weren't prepared the first time.

Another few days will be worth the wait, knowing that you can get all your homework done properly before the next time, and that you'll then wow them with a convincing and appealing approach that they can't say no to. And that's worth waiting for.

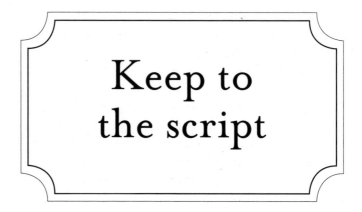

Keep to
the script

R ight, you've already made sure that you know exactly what you're asking for. However, you also need to know why the other person should give it to you. So the thing to do now is to memorise three key reasons why they should say yes.

That's not the same thing as three reasons why *you* want the thing. Your potential babysitter may not in the least care whether you learn Italian. Or what job you're hoping to get as a result. They're far more likely to be persuaded by reasons such as – you'll owe them a big favour, you'll mow their lawn every Saturday and your mother is prepared to do it very occasionally so they won't be letting you down if they have to skip a week once in a while.

Your partner may love you just as you are, but they may see the sense in supporting your diet if you point out that it will make you feel more confident, you'll be far easier to be around if you don't have to watch them tucking into take-away curries or doughnuts and you'll be able to go for those long walks they enjoy if you're leaner and fitter.

Your boss needs to hear why you should get a pay rise: you exceeded your targets yet again, you're now fully versed in important software that you couldn't previously use and you have taken on additional responsibilities.

Now you have to make sure that when you ask you remember to state clearly these three reasons for saying yes, so the other person is in no doubt about the benefits of saying yes to you.

# Rehearse it

I'm guessing if you're reading this book that you may not be entirely comfortable with asking for important things. If you've followed all the guidelines in this book, you've given yourself the best possible chance – you've persuaded the other person they'd like to say yes, and you've made it as easy as possible for them. All you need now is a bit more confidence.

And confidence comes from knowing exactly what you're doing. So before you actually meet up, rehearse and rehearse and rehearse what you're going to say. Do it in front of a mirror, or with a friend if you can. Go over it until you really feel confident of what you're saying, and have the right phrases or figures on the tip of your tongue.

You're not trying to script this word for word. That could sound stilted, which would make you feel uncomfortable. You might script the odd few words but otherwise it's the gist you're clear about, and the actual words can come naturally. We need to make sure that even if you're nervous or stressed or anxious or under pressure, you don't miss out anything important that could make a difference to the other person's final answer. So rehearse until you know that you can:

- Remember everything you want to say, even under pressure.

- Recall your three key points.

- Recall specific phrases that you think will help put your case.

- Remember any vital facts and figures you may need.

Look, this is the moment you've been working towards for days, weeks, maybe months. You can't afford to blow it all by muffing your lines when you get there.

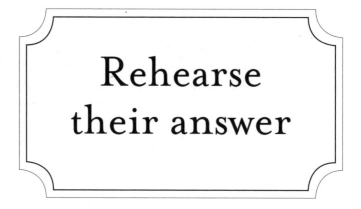

Rehearse
their answer

Right, you've rehearsed your lines, but what about theirs? What are *they* going to say? And actually, how can you have rehearsed all your lines without knowing how they'll react? Well you haven't, of course. You've rehearsed your opening gambit – you've practised how to put your case across. But once they respond you'll be clueless. You've no idea what they're going to say, so you'll be completely unprepared. If this is something big, they're hardly likely to say yes straight off, are they? They'll want to talk about it, ask questions, suggest alternatives, I don't know – anything might happen.

Well, not quite. It's true that you don't know exactly what they'll say, but you do have a pretty good idea of the options. After all, you've already thought through why they might say no, and what would help them to say yes. So if they don't give you a yes straight out, they're almost certainly going to come up with one of the objections you've already considered.

So you can actually prepare for this too, by rehearsing the counter-arguments you've prepared to their objections, until you're as solid on those as you are on your initial request. By the time you've thought through all the options, you'll find you've rehearsed their lines for them as well as your own. How thoughtful of you.

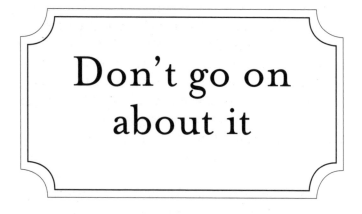

# Don't go on about it

So you've finally made it to the all-important meeting. You're sitting across from your boss – or whoever – and you're actually asking for what you want. You're making a clear case, putting across your three key points and showing them why they want to say yes.

When you get to the end of your rehearsed spiel, you pause. They're thinking about it. They don't react at once. So you take advantage of the pause to add another point, and then another, and another... Stop! Rewind! No, no, no – once you've said everything that needs to be said, shut up. Wait for them to speak next. The onus is on them so if they don't feel uncomfortable, you shouldn't.

The thing is, when you start speaking again the very least you do is interrupt their train of thought when they should be thinking about whether they can say yes to you. That's bad enough. But you could damage your case even further. Apart from irritating them (and we want them in a good mood, remember), you could confuse them with extraneous information. You've spent a lot of time making sure you are being clear and succinct, so don't risk becoming muddled and lengthy after all.

You might even put your foot in it inadvertently: '...and it won't jeopardise the TMK contract either'. Ah, the TMK contract. The boss had forgotten about that. Now you mention it, they're not so sure it won't jeopardise it. Hmmm. Maybe it's not such a good idea after all... You see? If you don't open your mouth, you can't put your foot in it.

Right, that'll do. I won't go on about it.

Get the
essentials on
paper

You've asked your boss, or the committee chairman, or the bank manager, a big question. They're going to have to think about it. Maybe talk it over with other people, or even get approval from someone more senior.

Of course you won't be there when that happens. So how are you going to make sure they do justice to your request? What if they forget the salient points? Fail to quote those crucial statistics that really clinch the argument? Get the baseline figures wrong? What indeed?

There's a very simple way round this. You just need to take a written summary to the meeting with you and hand it over. Keep it to less than a page, laid out well with headings, bullet points, lots of space. You know, so it looks easy to read quickly or get the key points from just by scanning. You're supposed to make this easy for them, remember. No one's going to bother to read a full sheet of close-typed text.

Think how reassuring that is. Whoever they talk to, or whenever they decide to think about their decision, you can be confident that they have all the facts and arguments they could need to hand, and you know they're accurate because you supplied them yourself.

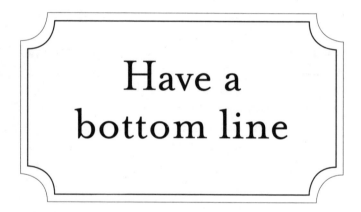

Have a
bottom line

Of course, once you've asked you may not get a straight answer. You may get a conditional one. In other words you'll have to negotiate. And when you've finished negotiating, you'll need to come away with something worth having.

Which is what, precisely?

You have to know the answer to this question, because otherwise you may find you've agreed to something that isn't actually any use to you. Before you start, you have to know what is the least you'll settle for. Whether you're buying a house, getting a pay rise, asking for a loan, or getting the builders in, if you don't know this before you start, you're in trouble.

And often it's not straightforward. Sometimes these things are a straight yes and no thing – how much are you prepared to pay for this car, for example – but in many cases there are lots of variables. You might settle for a smaller pay rise if there's a promise of a further raise next year. Depending on how much. And when next year. And if there are other perks to go with it. See? All these things can interrelate.

If the other person says maybe instead of yes you have to be ready to discuss these things, knowing that you won't fall into the trap of negotiating a deal that isn't worth it because you've got your bottom line fixed in your mind.

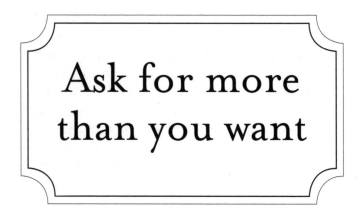

Ask for more
than you want

Some people will try to beat you down – you know they will. Remember the scene in Monty Python's *Life of Brian* where Brian is frantically trying to buy something from a market stall before his pursuers catch up with him. He tries to hand over the money and the stallholder refuses to deal with him unless he haggles over the price. Sometimes there's a good reason to negotiate you down, but a lot of people won't even need a reason.

So you start by asking for more than you want. Then, when they negotiate you down, you still end up where you privately hoped to be. Other people may be alarmed at the scale of what you're asking. When you drop what you're asking for they'll appreciate the concession and the final figure won't be so daunting. Suppose you want your sister to look after your children two days a week after school for an hour, until you get back from work. Ask her if she could manage three days. While she's thinking about it, let her know you can see this is a lot to cope with – maybe she could just do two days? By now, two days is looking far more manageable once she's contemplated three, and she's more likely to feel it's a reasonable request.

I'm not asking you to be manipulative, that's never a good approach. I'm assuming here that three days would be even better, but you can see that two is as much as you can reasonably ask. Don't ask for more than you'd accept – just for more than you expect or aim to get.

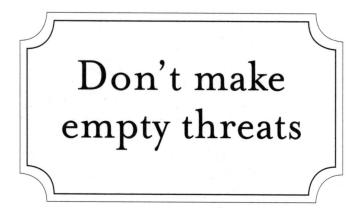

Don't make
empty threats

O r indeed any threats. That's not nice. But for your own sake don't say, imply, or threaten that if the other person doesn't do what you want you'll quit your job, or never help them again, or not be their friend, or never speak to them in the playground – well, that's how childish it is. Not only that, it's counter-productive.

For one thing they may call your bluff. You're going to feel pretty aggrieved if your boss says 'fair enough then, you'll have to find another job'. Now you've either got to do so, or lose face by staying anyway. And not only that – if you stay your boss now knows they can say no to you with impunity.

Threats cause bad feeling, and the other person is far more likely to say no to you next time if they're annoyed at being threatened this time. Your neighbour certainly isn't going to babysit for you ever again. Your mother won't reconsider her decision about the house move. And all those other things you might need them for in the future… you've blown it now.

Suppose the threat isn't empty? Suppose you really will leave your job if your manager won't give you a rise? Don't tell them – it will sound like blackmail however you play it. Just do it. When they say no, go and get another job, and when you hand in your notice you can explain – in regretful but polite terms – that you have had to take a job with better prospects. If losing you was ever going to change their mind, they'll make you an offer to get you to stay. If they don't, the threat wouldn't have worked (and wouldn't have helped your references either).

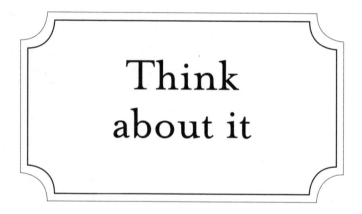

Think
about it

The negotiations have gone kind of OK. They haven't agreed to everything, but they have proposed a compromise. They'll lend you half the money; they'll give you a smaller pay rise than you wanted but they'll also give you other perks; they'll look after the kids every other week; they won't date you but they'll spend more time with you; they'll accept your offer but they won't do the repairs on the roof.

Hmmm. Is it worth it? That could be hard to say. In which case, don't say it. Don't feel rushed into making a decision, even if the other person is trying to pressure you. Listen, this is important. You can't spend all that time planning and then just blurt out a decision that is frankly no more than a guess. What if it turns out to be the wrong answer?

You always have the right to say, 'That's an interesting thought / proposal / idea / recommendation / offer. I'd like to think about it'. Then ask them when they want a response by, or make a suggestion yourself.

Now you have time not only to think, but also if necessary to collect more information to help you decide. Get a more accurate figure on the roofing costs, see if your sister could babysit on the alternating weeks, find out if there's any way to trim the budget further, analyse the savings you'll gain from working at home or having a company car. Once you've got all the facts in front of you, then you'll be able to go back with a clear decision that you know is the right one.

Put the decision in writing

**B**rilliant! They said yes! Congratulations. Now, let's just keep calm and think about this for a moment. Did they say yes unreservedly, or were there conditions? Did they agree the timing? Which one of you was going to double-check it with Matt? Will it still be OK for you to go on holiday in March?

And if you're sure you know all those answers, are you also sure that they do? And that you'll both still remember the same version the week after next? No, you can't be. Unless, of course, you write it down.

If there's a lot of detail to cover you need to take a notebook into the meeting with you. And, whether or not you've done that, if there's the slightest risk they could change their mind, or try to alter the conditions, or misremember the minutiae, you need to put it all down in writing afterwards. If it's a business meeting of some kind this will seem so normal you can just write it down with a covering note to say it seemed wise to put it down in writing. If that seems too formal you can still drop your neighbour a note, or your mum an email, to say, 'thanks so much for agreeing to look after the house while we're away. Here are the dates again for you, and it's such a relief to know the garden will be looked after too while we're gone'. There. Now if mum doesn't remember agreeing to weed the garden she can say so.

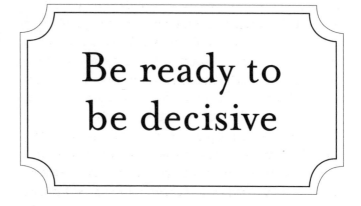

# Be ready to
# be decisive

You've done well getting this far, through all that planning and preparation. But what if they say no? If you've done your homework well it won't often happen, but inevitably there are times when you don't get what you set out to achieve.

Sometimes there's not a lot you can do but devise a Plan B and work towards that. If someone else gazumped you on the house you wanted, or your colleague got promoted over you, there's not a lot you do now. On the other hand, there are other houses and other jobs, and instead of giving up on the whole thing you can start planning for the next opportunity.

That's what the most successful people do. They work out what went wrong this time and they get cracking on the next challenge. Sometimes that can entail big decisions, and you have to be prepared for that. Maybe you just won't find a house that fits your requirements, and you have to decide what you'll compromise on. Perhaps your boss is never going to promote you and you need to look for another job. Maybe not, but you have to face up to the decision.

This is where the people who wait for answers to fall into their laps go wrong, and start to look unlucky. While the go-getters get going on Plan B and, sooner or later, get what they want without the need for luck.

So go back to the beginning (don't worry, a lot of the legwork's already done) and analyse what you need to do differently and whether that will entail making big changes. If it does, consider them carefully – don't hand in your notice in a fit of pique – and be prepared to try again or to be decisive about heading in another direction.

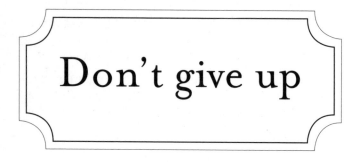

Don't give up

**M**aybe you're not willing to compromise, or you don't see the need. Maybe the answer isn't to jack in the job, or the marriage, or to move house, or enjoy being overweight. Maybe you still wanted what you started out wanting, and those things aren't the answer.

OK, then stick with Plan A. Quite right – sometimes big change isn't the answer. Sometimes you just need to keep at it. I lost count of the number of times I tried unsuccessfully to give up smoking. But I did it in the end. What if I'd given up trying to give up? Apart from the irony of it, I'd still be smoking now. The fact I'm not shows that persistence isn't futile.

Maybe you didn't get the promotion this time. But now that other candidate has moved on up, maybe you'll be the one next time – and meantime you can work on making yourself an even more promising applicant.

So no one would look after the kids while you went to Italian classes? They'll be starting a new course soon and maybe it will be on a better night. Or you'll find a parent at school who's happy to do a babysit swap with you every week. Or your partner will be able to get home early on a Thursday.

So don't quit[14]. Make challenging but realistic plans and work at making them happen. And whatever you do, don't rely on luck. In any case, if you're doing it properly, you won't need it.

[14] Apart from smoking.

**ALSO BY RICHARD TEMPLAR**, bestselling author of the globally successful *Rules* series.

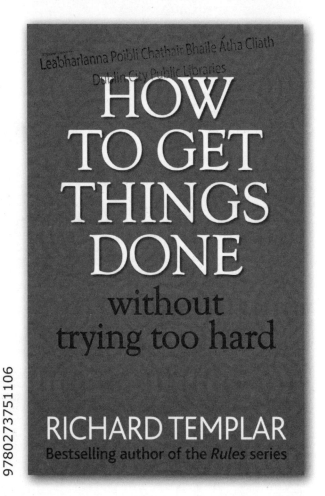

The world's most wise, witty and straightforward antidote to procrastination and guide to getting more done in less time.